HURRAH FOR THE VALLEY

Book II
(1938 – 1942)

KNUTE POWELL

ACKNOWLEDGEMENTS

A sincere thank you to my wife Claudia. As I write the second acknowledgement I know, that like everything I've ever accomplished, you helped make this book possible.

To Casey, Ryan, and Sean whose occasional readings and approval gave me the boost needed to complete this endeavor, a feeling of gratitude and pride.

No book can be written without an immense number of helpful friends, an editor, and advisors

Former "Duck" football player, and pride of the University of Oregon, Eric Elshire served as my editor. His contribution and literary skills proved extremely valuable. His high school students are lucky to have him for a teacher.

With the assistance of Steve Silcox, my college roommate and baseball fanatic, each baseball story was developed and described as the rules and situations demanded. His knowledge of baseball helped paint a picture of baseball, as it should be played.

Bob Welch, author of such great books as My Oregon, Easy Company Soldier: The Legendary Battles of a Sergeant From World War II's Band of Brothers, and many more, served as a mentor. His insightful instruction, and encouragement kept the dream of writing this book alive.

Author Jane Kilpatrick's notes, and knowledge she shared at the Beachside Writer's workshop proved valuable beyond belief. Reviewing her notes constantly led to needed revisions, and techniques that would have otherwise gone unchanged.

Without the assistance of Roger Hite, another U of O Duck, this book would have never made it to the printer. Roger was the calm in the storm whenever I began to panic with regard to formatting the manuscript, or getting the book printed.

To the families of Cullman, and Conley I can't express my appreciation enough for the use of your family journals, and letters. The narratives offered so much detail, and graphic portrayal of their lives that they themselves could have written this book. Clay, Clarence, and Joy Taylor offered the background on people, places, and events. They provided facts and time lines that allowed the narrative to be as realistic as possible. Thanks to my cousin Kim Wallis for taking the time from his civic duties to read some of the initial chapters. A high five to retired coach Bill Cooper, one of California's great coaches, for taking time from his family to read and make some much needed revisions.

I can't say thank you enough to Joe Holley and Pat Morrison. Joe shared his insights into baseball in Walker County. His endless trips to the library to sort out box scores, or to identify players and teams helped provide the validity my father and his brothers would appreciate. Pat's pictures of commissaries, tipple stations, schools, homes, and communities allowed me to create a picture of life in a mining town during the Great Depression. My father's reminisces of baseball players required some research. Thankfully, "baseball-reference.com" filled in the gaps.

Finally, a sincere thanks to Mrs. Frank Corry, Jane Teddy, Kelsey McMillan, Dr. Larry Powell, and all the others folks who took a long distance call from, or visited with, a total stranger. You provided direction leading to new resources. Many of you shared the details of a family member's life. I hope the book did justice to their memory.

"Talk to Your Brother"
by C.W. Powell

When you are growing up, and things get tough,
Talk to your brother, he's been through the rough.

When you feel down and out,
Talk to your brother, he knows what it's all about.

When your clothes don't fit, and you don't know
what to do,
Talk to your brother, he wore them before you.

When you feel locked out, and can't get in,
Talk to your brother, he is a your best friend.

When a friendly scuffle turns into a fight,
Talk to your brother, he knows what's right.

When your tired, and need some rest,
Talk to your brother, he knows what's best.

When you are lonesome, and don't know what to
say,
Talk to your brother, he will show you the way.

When you get older, and family grows thin,
Talk to your brother, he's your closest kin.

When you have lost your Father and Mother,
There is nothing like the love of a brother.

Chapter 1
"The Longest Triple"

"If you boys don't stop fighting and fussing with one another, I'm gonna tell your Pap to send you up to Earnest Chapel. Your Granddad and Uncle Fletch can put all that energy to work hoeing, picking cotton, and splitting firewood."

Momma threats to send us to Earnest Chapel to work for Granddad and our uncle brings the hostilities between Mote, my second oldest brother, to an abrupt standstill. We haven't been throwing punches, or gouging each other's eyes, but we have been threatening each other with insults, bumps, and elbows at every opportunity. Apparently Momma has heard enough. The dreadful notion of listening to Granddad's mournful accordion playing, or laboring at task that Uncle Fletch had been putting off for months quickly ends my vigorous insults and annoying elbowing on Mote. A whipping by Pap would be more welcome than spending time at Granddad's, and working for Uncle Fletch.

"Now get out of the house before you miss your ballgame. Just leave me and Precious some peace and quiet." Momma's promise to send us to Earnest Chapel is reason enough to get out of her sight quickly. Without a word between us, Mote and I grab our baseball mitts while Tut, who is a couple of years younger than me, snares two bats that Pap had made. With our gear in hand we head off to the ball field. Just in time. We have a game in Sipsey later today.

We haven't even closed the gate when Tut makes an observation about the warring between Mote and me that's been going on for several weeks. "You two are just edgy because Chip ain't around with some new adventure, or to settle your squabbles."

He hit the nail on the head with that one.

I have missed Chip's laugh, his solutions to any of my problems, his peace keeping in the family, and his enthusiasm for new adventures. Every time I'm on the ball field, I'm aware of someone else wearing his uniform. Baseball, it's the one thing that helps me get over Chip's departure for the Navy. Fortunately, I still have three siblings to play ball with, or join in some crazy antic to fill the summer days.

My other brother Deacon is coal mining over in Sipsey. So, he isn't around much. Joy, my baby sister ain't much into playing ball although she does smile, giggle, and scream at some of the antics that Mote, Tut, Jesse, and me pull to amuse her.

Pap and Momma have gotten several letters from Chip. He says the food is fine, but not as good as Momma's. He notes that for the first time that he can recall, he always has enough to eat. Not having to share a bed with a brother has been a true luxury of Navy life too. While he's figuring out all the rules the Navy has for sailors, he also writes about the schooling and the physical training. Apparently the physical training doesn't compare with playing football for Oakman.

Chip wants me to write and tell him how the Valley baseball team is doing. I hope I've got good news after today's game. We're playing on Sipsey's field and we're not taking their team lightly, not with the Julian brothers in the line-up. Bobby, Buck, and John Julian hold down three of the top five spots in their batting order. The Julian trio has helped the Sipsey team win all, but two games in May. There are conflicting stories circulating around the county that Sipsey beat the Barons in a practice game two weeks ago. Rumor is the Barons manager had taken a real shine to the Julian boys. He'd even invited the older boys to spring training next season. Now, Sipsey is undefeated coming into the second week of June.

"Can I go to the game?" Jesse, our little brother trails us to the ball field.

"No. Ain't room in the Roadster or the trailer. Besides, Momma said you ain't ever to ride in Mule's trailer." Jesse appears not to have heard a word of Mote's reply as he continues to walk in our shadows.

Mule, our team manage is already at the field when we arrive. Jesse seizes the opportunity, "Mule, can I got to the game?"

Before anyone can squash the idea, Mule tells Jesse to, 'Run home and ask your Momma.'

Jesse is grinning when Mule stops by the Commissary to pick him up, and squeeze him in between Mote and Runt in the rumble seat. My little brother loves baseball as much as our brothers and me.

Deacon is sitting behind the backstop, and next to him is a pretty girl. Her hair is glowing as the sun reflects off her blond waves. Deacon has spoken of her when he's been back to the Valley. Her name is Juanita.

This will be the first game Deacon has seen the Valley play this season as he's working for Sipsey Mine. I'm excited that he's here to watch our Valley team. A loud "Hurrah for the Valley" cheer signals that Ol' Reese, driving his horse drawn wagon, has arrived. Sheriff Cox has ridden over from the Valley for the game and sits, mounted, on his big red horse near the third base foul line.

Like all Walker County folks, the people in Sipsey are serious about their baseball. The Sipsey field is a fine place to play ball, as the infield is smooth as a checkerboard while the outfield grass is as thick as bristles on a woman's hairbrush. Looking about the field, my attention is drawn to right field. There is no fence, only a grassy hill that starts slopping up about 300 feet from home plate. At the top of the gentle slope, another 100 feet away, sits the yellow brick Sipsey schoolhouse.

While the ball field is first rate, the Sipsey team wears the customary uniform of over-all's and a variety of caps. Some of their players are barefoot too. With our warm-ups complete we watch the Sipsey team go through their pre-game ritual. Mule comments on the various throws of each Sipsey player, drawing attention to each Sipsey player's ability to field balls hit to his the right or left.

Our attention shifts from the field to a white, green and black truck pulling up near the ball field. Immediately I recognize the "Birchfield Theater" truck that had passed through Oakman the day we saw Chip off for his Navy training. Seated in the truck is the same young driver that announced the movies. Mote takes notice of the truck.

"Birchfield looks to be a baseball fan too?"

"Plaaaay Ball." The umpire is a pale, mature, looking fellow. His thin, sandy colored hair is combed to one side. He's skinny as a fence post. A white shirt, black bow tie, and black trousers identify his trade. The umpire is the local preacher. Mule has inserted Runt, playing second base, into the leadoff spot. Runt thumps his spikes with the bat, steps into the batters box, and taps the far side of the plate. He finally settles into his semi crouching stance.

"What a grand day for baseball. Folks, it doesn't get any better in Walker County.

Folks, I'm Noel Passé, and I'm announcing the game courtesy of Birchfield Theaters."

The amplified voice of this Passé fellow startles the Sipsey pitcher, one of the Julian brothers. Distracted, he steps back off the mound. The umpiring preacher, standing behind the mound, looks from one side of the field to another. Every ballplayer in the field and on the benches is craning his neck in the direction of the white truck and it's large loudspeakers.

"Now batting for the Valley, Earnest, playing second base." "Why it's just like watching the Barons, or St. Louie," someone sitting behind the backstop utters, "Ain't it the berries?"

Now that he's apparently decided that the game's announcement is more of a treat than a disturbance the umpire again roars "Plaaaaay Ball".

Runt takes the first pitch for a strike, or "Breezed him" as the voice in the truck announces. The second pitch to Runt yields a high chopper. The shortstop waits for an eternity before the ball settles down in his glove. Runt has scampered safely to first base.

"That Baltimore Chop gives the Valley the first base runner of the day," blares the voice from truck.

Two pitches later the lightening quick Runt is off. Johnny Cicero, our burly outfielder, is batting. Runt's spikes are kicking dirt high into the afternoon sky. His slide sends up a red cloud as he swipes second base.

One pitch later, Mule, suspecting the game to be a close one, has Cicero lay down a bunt that leaves the Sipsey third baseman, another Julian, only one option, a throw to first base for an out. Runt is now in position to score from third base.

The sound of hearing "Now batting" along with my name seizes my body with a burst of excitement. I freeze on the first pitch.

"Julian chunked that one by him," echoes in my ears.

I step away from the plate. I take a few slow, quiet, breaths, and study the line of thin clouds slowly gliding high above the ridges. With a sense of calm I take three swings, step back up to the plate. The only sound I hear is the Sipsey catcher slapping his large, over-stuffed, glove as he settles in behind me. I know he is chattering, but that too, falls on deaf ears. My sole focus is Julian's release point. It's another straight pitch, inside, and chest high. The right fielder races to retrieve my line drive as it rolls to the base of the hill. The shortstop is still waiting for the relay throw from the second baseman when I slide in for a double. Runt scores.

Our one run lead holds up until the fifth inning when the Julian brothers mount a brief rally that gives the Sipsey team a two run lead. The score remains 3 – 1 in the final inning. Runt is on first, and Bud Millwood standing at second.

As I hustle to the plate, eager for my ups, I hear Deacon calling from behind the backstop where he is still camped on the wooden bleachers.

"Hit a homerun, and I'll buy you any bat you want in Jasper."

I clinch my jaw in an attempt to force the smile of my face. On the third pitch I feel the ball shudder on the impact with my bat.

Sprinting toward first I sneak a quick peek at the soaring ball. The ball lands, bounces and then collides with the yellow brick schoolhouse. Sprinting around the bases, Deacon's incentive rattles around in my brain with every step. Then, I begin to laugh. Reaching third base, I'm laughing so hard that I stumble and fall. Still laughing, I regain my feet and rush toward home. The catcher and the ball are waiting for me. Deacon won't be buying me a bat anytime soon.

"Folks, ya just seen the longest triple ever hit in Walker County."
Seems like everyone is laughing now, except me.

At this moment I don't appreciate this Passe fella, and his baseball lingo, too much.
The score is tied for two more innings when Jack drives Mote home from second with a two out poke deep up the right field slope.

"Hurrah for the Valley" rings in the air. The Sipsey folks aren't any too pleased with Ol' Reese and his cheering.

With the game over, Deacon, with Juanita holding his arm, finds me. I'm filling my mouth with an egg sandwich. "Ya almost cost me half a day's wages with that last poke."

" A Jimmy Foxx model wouldn't be cheap."

Deacon nods, "Spike, this is Juanita. Juanita this is Spike, the best hitter in The Valley."

"Hello." The perky Juanita and I exchange greetings and a short handshake.

"Someday they'll be paying him to put his name on Louisville bats."

I don't know how to respond as Deacon slaps my back. We talk about Momma and Pap and then Deacon and Juanita wander over to visit with Mote, Mule, and the other Valley players.

Looking around the field I spot the youngest Julian visiting with Jack. I drift over to join their conversation. They're talking about the Sipsey game with the Barons.

"Playing Sipsey would be easier if all you Julian's hurry and catch on with the Barons". Jack laughs, and then adds, "Be a blessing for every county team."

John Julian smiles. "Maybe Bobby and Buck, but someone has to stick around to see you Coal Valley boys don't bust up the schoolhouse with line drives."We chat for a few more minutes before shaking hands and rejoining our teammates.

Hustling, Jack and I jump aboard the trailer that's hitched to the rear of Mule's Ford. Mule built the trailer out of an old wagon. He'd removed the two front wheels from the creaky, weathered, wagon. He then attached the pine wagon tongue to the bumper of his roaster using some long bolts.

Riding in Mule's trailer is as thrilling as some of the carnival rides that come to the county. We bounce and bump in the long, dusty, trailer ride back to The Valley. The trip is a bruising journey. Seated in the trailer, my attempt to steer the conversation to Jack's crucial hitting and Mote's savvy base running are in vain. The team continues to find amusement in my base running exploits.

Our backsides ache from the trailer ride when we arrive back in the Valley. Once we unload, Jack accompanies Mote and me on the slow march up the pitch-black road toward home. The stiffness brought on by the trailer ride home quickly fades. The smell of Momma's cooking grabs our attention as we set foot on the porch. Momma has fried okra, biscuits, and bacon simmering on the stove.

"Jack, you'd best join these two for supper. No sense in your sister's having to fend for you this time of day."

"Thank ya Mrs. Powell." Momma gets no argument from Jack.
"Evening fella's." Pap strolls in as Momma sets out supper. He'd just finished his evening smoke on the back porch.

"Good evening, Pap", or "Mr. Powell" circles the table.

Pap says Grace, and then proceeds to look around the table. "Sheriff Cox stopped by for a spell." His facing registers a smile, his eyes are twinkling like stars in the night sky. I know he has a story to tell. His eyes settle on me.

"Sheriff said he'd seen the longest ball ever hit in Walker County over in Sipsey today. He said, "If some fella could learn how to put one foot in front of the other, he'd sure be one fine ballplayer."

For the first time in my life I pretend I don't hear Pap. I attack my supper while Mote and my pal, Jack, stop eating, laughing too hard to swallow.

Chapter 2
"Ya Want to Start Over?"

The dirt around the house looks smooth as if Momma had ironed it. I admire my work like Ruth watching a home run. Mote, with his mitt, mask, and chest protector bundled over his shoulder, urges me to "Get the lead out" as he sails out the front door and off the porch. He's running as if the devil is chasing him. His destination is the Commissary where the team is loading up for the trip to Townley for today's game.

Whether by mule pulled wagons, sorry looking trucks, or by saddleback, you name it, folks are flocking to see our Valley baseball team. Ol' Reese says he reckons a thousand folks watched the last game. It was a rematch with the Julian brothers and Sipsey. Old Reese says he gained substantial benefits from putting his trust in The Valley baseball team.

With my task finished, and antsy to join the team, I flash through the house collecting my spikes, glove, and bat from under the bed. I stop in the kitchen where Momma has set out golden brown biscuits, dripping with her fig preserves. I grab two before busting out the door.

"You numbskull."

Barefoot and jumping up and down with both feet Tut is creating a dust storm in front of the house. My freshly swept yard looks as if pigs had been rooting in it.
Tut is panicked by my outburst. Quickly realizing that his life's in danger if I get my hands on him, Tut attempts to escape into the road. I cut off his retreat as my right foot catches his skinny little bottom a few steps short of the gate.

Tut's short flight, across the yard, ends with an "Ugh."
Scrambling to his feet, blood begins to trickle from a small cut
on his forehead.
"How many times I gotta warn ya to stay out of the front
yard? You think Momma has me sweeping so you can make
dust storms the likes of the Dust Bowl?"

Clinching the straps of his homemade over-alls in my hands I
impress upon Tut that I take my chores seriously.
"Sorry. Sorry Spike, I'll fix it."

"No. I'll do it. I want it done right. You best find another place
to live if Mule leaves without me, because you'll be cruisin for
a bruisin."
I run back to Pap's shed to collect my yard broom. Tut is
nowhere in sight when I get back to the front yard. Frantic, I
dance around the front yard, brushing with whirlwind speed.
I remove any trace of Tut's antics as I restore the yard to its
pristine state.
I return the broom to the shed, grab my baseball gear and race
off to the Commissary. I'm frantic. Has the team left without
me?

Whew. Mule's 34' Roadster, with the wooden trailer bolted to
the rear bumper, still stands in front of the Commissary. My
spikes, draped around my neck, sway and bump across my
body. My pace quickens. Charging like Sergeant York I cradle
the bat with my glove hooked around the barrel in both hands
as my teammates yell.

"Come on Spike."

"Let's go."

"Get the rocks out of your pockets." His fingers are tapping the steering wheel. Mule's expression is either one of relief, or agitation. The two Cicero brothers and Bud Millwood join Mule in the Roadster. To my disappointment, Berl and Mote already occupy the rumble seat. Tossing my gear aboard, I scramble into the trailer. I settle in next to Jack and Conky who is Mule's latest addition to the team. The trailer lunges forward causing me to tumble onto Conky and Jack. Mule eases off the clutch and puts his foot to the accelerator. We leave the Commissary bathed in the red Valley dust.

For the first few miles of the trip the talk is about the St. Louis Browns. Conky professes that if not for Harlond Clift, our Valley team is pert near as good as the Browns. Pine boughs and massive limbs of oak trees form a tunnel overhead. The shade offers some relief from the blistering summer rays.

As we approach the steep grade of Wyndom Hill our conversation moves to the Townley game. We share stories of a killing, and fights involving visiting teams and Townley fans.

Conky feeds more fuel to the fire, "Yep, Daddy said it was ten years ago. It was a big fight between the Townley folks and the Sipsey team; fists flying and swinging bats. Lucky no one got killed that time. Yes Sir, best not be sassing any Townley folks today."

The trailer bounces and sways as we start down Wyndom Hill when a thundering, Crack, then a Pop, and another Crack halts all the talking. The crashing sound of a tree snapping in a windstorm has us hunting for the source of broken wood. "It's the wagon tongue."

Runt, his face contorted and white, is seated at the front of the trailer. He is pointing down to where the pine tongue connects to Mule's Roadster.

At the top of his lungs Runt roars, "The tongue broke."

I see Berl and Mote seated in the rumble seat. Their eyes are frozen like big saucers as they watch the trailer. The trailer is gaining speed as it threatens to climb up the rear end of the speeding Ford.

The trailer is cracking and groaning with every bumps and bounce. It twists like leaves in the wind. I grab hold of the trailer's sideboards, and watch Berl hammer his fist on the roof of the Roadster.
Cries of "Mule, Mule," and "Stop" fill the wind.
Someone is praying. It's me.

The trailer is inches away from slamming into the rear of Mule's Ford when it veers to one side. I feel like I'm flying. We sail up the side of a cut-bank. A jarring collision in a thicket of small pines tips and flips the trailer. I see the sky, tree limbs, dirt, and the sky again. I tumble like a wounded bird. The ground abruptly ends my flight through the thicket.

Laying on the ground my mind is full of whirling stars. Calls for Runt, Conky, Hop, Jack, Spike, fill the hillside. I'm alive. Rolling to my knees, I stagger to my feet. The scene looks like a picture of a battlefield. Bodies, the broken trailer, and baseball gear are scattered across the hillside.
"Ugh. Youch. Eeeeeeeee" reveal the locations of wounded teammates. Mule and the occupants of the Roadster are scrambleing over the hillside.

Like a dream the team begins to rise from the dust. Mule takes a quick survey of the carnage. Looking around I count bodies. We're all here, standing and alive.
"Well ain't we a fine looking team?"

Again I appraise my teammates. I see bloody noses and lips, facial cuts, cat like scratches, and dirty faces. Conky has blood in his scalp. The taste of dirt and blood mingle in my mouth. Everywhere I look I see torn over-alls and traces of blood.

My glove, my spikes, the Barons baseball cap, Pap's homemade bat, where are they? In a frenzied state I begin searching for my most prized possessions. Like prospectors searching for gold the team scurries around the wrecked trailer searching for baseball gear. I find all my treasured gear. My glove was still resting in the demolished trailer.
Like a large animal the trailer lies on one side. One spinning wheel remains on the trailer. As it continues to spin I'm reminded of a wounded animal struggling to survive. Severely damaged and no longer fit to ride, the trailer will probably serve for kindling in the months ahead. Assessing the condition of his trailer, and our options, Mule ask if anyone wants to head back to The Valley?

"Heck, all we got are bumps and bruises."
"Shoot, I'd been hurt more just feeding the chickens."

"My little sister beat me up something fierce too."

"Hurrah for The Valley, that's what Reese would be saying."

"Ya want them folks over in Townley thinking poorly of us."

"Heading home only means Momma having chores for me."

Runt squeezes into the rumble seat with Berl and Mote. Conky has piled into the Ford with Mule, Bud, Gus, and Johnny. Hop straddles a front fender. Jack and I stand on the running boards where we hold on to the open window frames. The wind cools the cuts and scratches that mar my face, neck, and arms.

"Let's play ball."

Dust once again fills the sky as the packed Roadster barrels down the road. Our arrival in Townley is greeted with great fanfare.
"Lordy. What in heaven's name happened to you boys?"
"Mule drag you boys behind that fancy car?"

"Them Valley uniforms sure fine looking."

"Your Momma let you leave home looking like that?"

Jeers, fits of laughter, and hoots pelt us. The jovial insults continue throughout our warming up. We are a sorry looking bunch.

The Townley ball field is smack dab in the middle of the company town. Two buildings shadow first and third base. One is a company store. The other is a rock structure. The fortress looking building has a second story. The only window is on the second floor. The only door is iron like the cast iron door on a potbelly stove.

"It's a jail. They got themselves a jail on the ball field. I told ya that folks here in Townley don't cotton to getting whooped. Why they even put you in jail if you beat'em." Conky continues to rant and fret about the jailhouse as Townley takes the field. Townley's white uniforms are so bright it's all I can do to look at them. The sleeves are red as are the letters spelling out "Townley" on the front of their shirts.
Mote is appraising our opponent. "Why ain't they a pretty sight?"

Sitting on the plank that serves as a bench, watching the Townley team go through their warm-up, I see a familiar figure approach the field. His frame and facial features are so slight I imagine his bones rattling as he walks. His long strides are easy. Yet, he carries himself with a sense of importance like a school principal, judge, or revenuer. Despite the oppressive heat and the sticky humidity the man is wearing a black store bought suit complete with tie, vest, and coat. A black fedora sits on his head. A thickly rolled half smoked cigar is clinched between his teeth. The old stogie constantly traverses from one side of his mouth to another. The suit hangs on the fellow like clothes hung out to dry.

"That fella sure looks familiar." Mote wedges his body in between Runt and me. "Who does he think he is, Connie Mack?

Sure enough, I do know him. That's Uncle Wiley. Mote calls him Uncle Wiley, but he isn't what you call blood kin. In Walker County if you're kin, or kin of kin, you're either uncle or aunt somebody. I'd recall meeting him once over in Earnest Chapel when he was visiting with Granddad and Grandma. Boy, is he a dandy looking manager.

The umpire apparently decides that it's time to parley. Uncle Wiley beckons Mule to join him. The umpire wears both tan trousers and shirt. A black tie is loose around his neck. Around his waist the umpire wears a black belt and holster. The badge on the front pocket tells me that the umpire is the local sheriff.
"That's a fine kettle of fish. The umpire is the sheriff. Now, ain't that peachy. Ya getta hit, go in high busting up a double play, or strike out one of his kin, then fast enough to make your head spin you're watching the game from jail." Conky is one worrywart when it comes to baseball in Townley. The meeting between the three men is over.

Mule calls us together. "Mr. Wiley say's as we've come so far, and had a tough journey, we don't need no coin flip, we're batting first. That Mr. Wiley sure seems awful sure of himself. These Townley boys think the sun comes up so they can crow in the morning."

Any notion the Townley boys had of winning today vanishes quick as a wink. It's still the first inning and I'm batting for the third time. The pitch is in my wheelhouse and I stroke my third double of the day. Runt, and Johnny cross home plate. The score is now 19 – 0.

"Time."

Uncle Wiley is making his way over to the umpire. Maybe Conky's right, I might be thrown in jail.

"Mule, we need to visit." Our manager eases his way out to the middle of the infield to join the umpire and Uncle Wiley.

"Ya all want to start over?"

Standing on second base I'm fixing to laugh when I hear Uncle Wiley's plea for a new game.
"I don't see why not." Mule turns and waves me off the field.
"We're batting first again."

Townley's prayers for a new outcome go unanswered. Mule and Uncle Wiley agree after the second game reaches the fourth inning that we'd best get back to the Valley. Our team hustles over to the fried chicken and sweets that have been set out for the spectators and players.

Fried chicken? Townley must have been expecting to be on the other end of that shellacking. The Townley team sure didn't appear to have much of an appetite as they quickly wander off.

Shoving a slice of honey lathered cornbread into his mouth while waving a drumstick, Mote ventures that every Valley player had scored at least three times in the second go around.

With our mouths full, we crowd into and on Mule's Roadster for the trip back over Wyndom Hill. The trip is jovial until we come upon the broken remains of the trailer. The road is now as quiet as an empty church as our laughter and voices grow silent. With the gears shifted down, the Roadster creeps by the remains of the trailer. It's busted and twisted body lies like a dead horse near the road. The only sound is the Roadster's tires crunching the hardscrabble road and rocks thudding against the fenders. Our team is hushed. Each player is lost in his own thoughts.

Mote breaks the silence, "Hey Mule, ya' all want to start over."

I'll bet the folks in Townley can hear our team as we bust out laughing. I'm laughing so hard my stomachaches. I don't think I'll ever forget the laughing faces of my teammates.

Chapter 3
"A Bag of Tricks"

Summer is just a few short weeks past. Yet, it feels like I've been going to high school all my life. Still, I've enjoy the early challenge of high school. I'm a member of the football team. Plus, I've met boys and girls from Oakman, making new friends. Still, autumn always leaves me with mixed feelings. I miss baseball, the games, practice, riding with Mule and the team around Walker County.

A World Series match up between the two New York teams allowed me to savor the game for a few more days. My pals and me were whooping it up when Ivy Andrews, a ballplayer that grew up in Dora, pitched for the Yankees in the World Series. The Series already has me looking forward to getting back on the field and battling the teams from Empire and Gorgas. Those teams had proven tough customers for every other Walker County team.

Mote is convinced that Empire and Gorgas were loaded up with professional players from the Sally League, posing as miners, during the season.

"Fact is, none of them ballplayers ever stepped foot in any coal mine." Mote swears that Old Reese has learned that a "Heap of players had no notion of coal mining." I'm itching for the next summer, and a new baseball season.

With the autumn winds comes a different excitement. Halloween is coming. Plans for Halloween have created new and daring tricks. My younger brothers are proving to be chips off the old block when it comes to planning some new form of mayhem for the folks in the Valley.

Every night for the past three days, Jesse and our cousin Lynn have been hunting the roads preparing for Halloween. Lynn, Uncle Rich's youngest, has become Jesse's new pal. The wavy haired Lynn is tall for his age and thin as a rake. The new pals are a pair to be reckoned with when it comes to games and mischief. Jesse is set to reveal the object of their nightly prowls to me whilst fetching coal near the Black Creek trestle.

"Come on" he urges. Toting Momma's kitchen coal, I follow Jesse home. I deposit the bag of coal on the back porch and then sprint to catch up with my youngest brother who's jumped the fence that surrounds the garden and is making fast tracks up the hill.

Out of breath, we're near the top of the ridgeline where Jesse pulls to a stop at a large oak tree. Suspended from a thick limb are six tote sacks. Jesse scampers up the tree, scoots out on the large limb and removes one of the sacks. Whatever Jesse has in the sack, it or them, is squirming.
Dropping to the ground, Jesse handles the sack as if it contains dynamite. He peers inside, and then holds out the sack. "Here take a peek. Ya best be careful."

Jesse's tentative behavior, and warning, has me leery and suspicious of the sack's contents. The notion that the sack is full of snakes leaves me cautious.

I ease the top of the sack open and begin to peek inside when an odor like a ball field privy, rises from the sack. The smell alone causes me to flinch. Skunk? No, I know skunk, and this is no skunk. Holding my breath, I look inside the sack.
Possum.
"What're you doing with this critters?"

"Lynn, and me, we're fixin' a Halloween surprise."

"How did ya come to get so many?"

24

"We'd be on the road, quiet like, and when one crosses the road, we thump them with a stick. They'd just roll up into a ball. We'd grab the tail and drop it into the tote sack." Again the stench rose from the sack. "Whew. How you stand to fetch them?"

"Didn't smell to bad at first, then they started peeing in the sack"

Sensing that whatever Jesse is planning, I'm better off not knowing should their plan backfire. The less I know, the better. Tomorrow is Halloween, so folks are sure to be wary of any boys sneaking around The Valley once darkness falls.

"Best not let Mr. Dutton, or Sheriff Cox catch you. Pap finds out you been
tricking, you'll be cutting a switch for sure."

"If the shoe fits, wear it. I heard you all talking about Halloween. Tut's said, 'This Halloween fixin' to be the grandest ever.'

"Best you mind who listening when you start talking about Halloween."

Halloween night the sky is as dark as an abandoned mine. Like a carnival, Halloween promises to bring a heap of excitement and amusement. Tut, Pud, Conky, and Shorty Schultz have come up with a trick for Halloween. Mote and I decide to join in their little escapade. Not to be left out, Runt and Berl join in on the adventure too. We head over to the Company garage where, tucked in behind the shop, is our objective. Old Reese keeps the large wooden wagon he uses for hauling trash at the site. Tut had come up with a Halloween trick that will surely have folks talking in the morning.

Runt, Berl, and Shorty have rounded up a variety of tools. With the aid of the tools, and elbow grease, we manage to pull the wheels from the wagon. We disconnect the wagon tongue, and remove the large box seat. It takes us several trips between the Company shop and the ball field to move the wagon, piece by piece, to our staging area.

Once we have the disassembled wagon at the ball field, we improvise a relay to get the dismembered wagon across the road and into the shadows of the massive building. Frequent stops are required as we constantly halt and attempt to lay low, encountering other tricksters heading up to Silk Stocking Road for sweets.

My hands are bleeding from my effort to roll the heavy wheel across the road. The biggest building on the road is quiet, as Uncle Cullie has left a few lights burning in hopes of discouraging any tricks to the Company store. Crouching in the shadows, we huddle in the darkness to plot our next step.

We gather at one end of the porch. Tut reveals a rope and pulley that Old Reese uses for hefting heavy loads into the wagon. Mounted on Berl's shoulders, Runt is hosted up to the porch roof, and attaches the pulley to one of the large beams that serves as a stringer between the roof and the Commissary. With the pulley secure we assemble at the loose end of the rope. The other end is now attached to a couple of the wagon wheels. We groan, and the pulley squeals, as we strain to get the large, wooden wheels level with the porch roof. The roof must be ten to twelve feet above the road. Grunting, and puffing, we manage to get the wheels on the roof. We work with military precision as we repeat the taxing maneuver until the entire wagon sits on the roof. Our backs, shoulders, and arms ache. Our caper is still undetected as we set to work patching the wagon back together.
Once the task is complete Runt removes the pulley, and tosses it into the wagon.

Now, with the prank complete we beat a hasty path to the Black Creek railroad trestle. There we collapse, beaten to the point of exhaustion.

Tut is beside himself. "Boy, won't folks be having a fit once they see Old Reese's wagon come tomorrow morning?"

White teeth glisten in the darkness as smiles break out on our faces. Once we recover from the burden of posing our trick, and our escape, we head out to see what treats are still to be had up on Silk Stocking Road. I'm delighted when Shorty's momma comes to the door with a pecan pie. Once we thank her, and we return to the road, my piece of pie is only a memory. Here, on the road, we assure each other that we will appear as innocent as newborn babes.

Mote, Tut, and I decide to return to the house, one at a time, figuring we'll cause less commotion. Pap is sure to have a heap of questions if we saunder in together.
Arriving home first, I find Pap and Momma sitting and rocking in the front room. To my surprise Jesse is home. Apparently his mystery trick is complete.

"Suppose you've been embarrassing the family name tonight?" Before I can respond, Pap encourages me to get washed up and hit the hay. Pap greets Mote and Tut's arrival in a similar manner.

Our room is dark as my brothers and I are lying in bed. We're talking about the tricks we had employed earlier this evening. "Mailboxes? You put possum in folk's mail boxes?" Mote is stifling a laugh. Tut is almost suffocating as he presses the pillow over his face. Jesse is revealing the trick that he and Lynn had pulled tonight.

"Put one in the Deputy's sedan too."
"Lordy, ya lucky ya'all didn't get shoot."

"You boys got so much energy, maybe we should find some nighttime chores for you."

As Pap's voice carries through the house, we pull the homemade quilts over our heads. Except for a few giggles the remainder of the night is uneventful.

Momma's breakfast of eggs and grits signals the start to another day. Everyone is anxious to head off to school. More importantly, I want to know how last night's trick with the trash wagon is being handled over at the Commissary?

Packing biscuits and school books, and dressed in hand-me-downs, we trudge off to school. Mote and I will catch the high school bus at the Commissary. We've just passed through the gate when Tut shouts,

"Look at the folks around the Commissary."

Like Tut, I take quick notice of folks standing around the Company store. Mote's attention is also drawn to the small crowd,

"Only see this many people at church on Christmas morning."

Uncle Cullie is wearing his white shop apron. His hands are set firmly on his hips. He walks around, peering up at the wagon. His footsteps beat a path back and forth as he paces past the porch. He shakes his head while a look that borders on frustration and bewilderment is displayed on his broad face.

Like cats, we slide into the crowd, listening to the conversations.

"Holy cow, how you figure they got Reese's wagon upon the porch?"

"Must've taken half the kids from the school."

"Had to be a bunch of miners over from Sipsey way. No way youngsters manage a stunt like this one."

"Dang. Ain't that the darnest trick ya ever seen?"

We continue to circle the crowd. We listen to the great acclaims for our Halloween trick.
"Look. Here comes Old' Reese"
Hopping up on the Commissary porch I can see Reese Edinburg hustling down the road. His black coat is worn over his over-alls. The coat tails flapping like a horsetail slapping flies. His trademark cigar set firmly in the corner of his mouth. Old Reese has company. Big John is heading to the Commissary too.

"Morning Reese. Looks like the trash business is late today."

"Strange place to leave your wagon Reese."
The crowd is taking great delight in our trick. The crowd grows quiet as Old Reese survey's his wagon, and it's awkward location.

Old Reese and Uncle Cullie come together like generals plotting their next campaign. They shake their heads, point at the roof, and shake their heads some more.
"Isn't that Jim Dandy." My brothers and pals are gathered around me.

"Best trick we'd pulled since Mr. Dutton fell in the outhouse.

Beep. Beep. Beep.

The sound of the school bus horn sends a panic through our small group. Reverend Graber is the minister at the Church of Christ in Oakman. He also drives the school bus. A big man, his face is creased from his frequent smiles. Reverend Graber always knows who's in need of a blessing, or a prayer. He can answer any question about Scripture. He is waving us over to the bus.

I realize that all the kids who ride the bus to Oakman are captivated by the best trick ever. They too are unaware of Reverend Graber's arrival. I follow my schoolmates as we scramble aboard the well-traveled bus.

The bus, bouncing and swaying, is soon moving along Oakman Road. Passing Coal Valley School, I see Tut, Jesse, and their pals, hustling to the schoolhouse. Mr. Dutton stands at the door. The students are lining up as they preparing for his command, "March In." Mr. Dutton looks like he survived Halloween again this year.

"Oh, Oh." Mr. Cox is sitting on his horse, next to the schoolhouse. Why is the sheriff at the schoolhouse? Jesse? Possums? Lord, help my little brother. The appearance of the Sheriff at the school a day after Halloween can't be a coincidence. Someone is fixing to get his or her bottom licked. Sure as shoot'in.

Like cold molasses, the school day creeps along. I fret about Jesse, his possum's, and the Sheriff all day. School is over when Reverend Graber drops us off at the Commissary.

"It's gone." Mote's words stun me like cold water. How? The wagon is not on the porch roof.

My feet waste no time once they touch the road as I sprint for home. The trash wagon is no longer important as I think of my little brother in jail.

I'm relieved to find Jesse in the back yard. He has exchanged his school over-alls for the faded, ragged ones he wears when not in church, or school. He's bouncing a rubber ball off the steps, and snags it on the rebound.

"Hi ya Spike." Without missing a bounce, Jesse continues to fire the ball at the porch steps.

"Why did Sheriff Cox come to the schoolhouse this morning?" The throwing, and catching, immediately comes to a standstill.

"Mr. Corry showed up too."

"Mr. Corry, the Oakman postmaster?"

"Yep."

"Why they come to school"

"Mr. Dutton had all the boys come to the lunch room for a meeting with Mr. Corry, and the Sheriff. Mr. Corry says that 'hindering the delivery of the mail is against the law.' Said the government will send feds to arrest the folks that messed with the delivery of the mail. He said who's ever putting dangerous animals in a mailbox could be sent to prison. Mr. Corry said that Mrs. Roberts almost passed out when she went to deliver the mail early this morning when a possum come flying out of the mailbox soon as she opened it. Took her a spell to regain her senses. He said the poor woman was a nervous wreck by the time she had opened the next five mailboxes."

"Is Sheriff Cox looking for those hindering with the mail?"

"No. He was investigating as to who had put a possum in the patrol car. He said, 'The car stunk something fierce, and them that put the possum in the car were interfering with the duties of a police officer.' Sheriff said he expected to be making an arrest real soon."

"I sure hope you and Lynn ain't suspects?"

"You think I should hide out with Grandpa over in Cordova?"

"Maybe the Sheriff will catch them possum and get them to talking. Until then, I think you're safe".

Chapter 4
"Deacon's Car"

"It cost me ten dollars."

Deacon is telling Pap, my brothers and me, how much he'd paid for the car he bought in Sipsey. Deacon's 1925 Chevrolet Roadster is blue, with tires mounted on yellow spokes like those on a bicycle. The white canvas roof is shredded in several places, and when the wind blows the torn fabric rustles like cornhusks in September. A silver radiator, missing a cap, is mounted on the front of the car. The body of the car appears to have been beaten repeatedly with a hammer. Dents, which feel like Momma's scrub board, are scattered across the body. The right front fender is missing and the running board is twisted something fierce, like a piece of licorice candy.

Mote pulls his head out of the car. "When you'd learn to drive a car?"

"Learned to drive trucks in Sipsey. When the Company needed dynamite, or some trash
hauling, I went along to learn how to drive. Manager let me drive after a few trips." I sense the pride in Deacon's voice as he recounts his driving experience.

Pap lies on the ground examining more of the Chevrolet. "You got a heap of dirt caught up under the fenders."

"Man I bought it from had to pull it out of the ditch with his mules."

"How he'd come by this automobile?"

"State Police said if he'd fetch it out of the ditch he's welcome to it. The man said it belonged to a counterfeiter. Fella ran into a ditch trying to escape the police. Police told the man that the counterfeiter wouldn't be needing a car for a long spell."

Mote is examining the back of the car. "These bullet holes in the lid?"
We quickly huddle around Mote standing at the rear of the car, where he's investigating six, or seven, holes. "Yep, sure looks like bullet holes."

"Man said the counterfeiter and the police were shooting at each other."

"Counterfeiter get shot?"

"Man sold it to me said that fella got knocked out when he ran into the ditch."

"How come the man sold it?"
"Fella said he had two good working mules, and a nice mare for his buggy. Didn't see any need for an automobile."
"How does she run?"

"No problem getting her started. She heated up some over by Cordova. Had to stop at Grandpa's and fetch water for the radiator. One of the front wheels is bent from hitting the ditch. It wobbles some when I drive."

Deacon continued, "I heard there's a garage over in Jasper that been taking in automobiles that been wrecked, or been used to settle debts at the hardware store or mercantile. I'm driving over there first thing tomorrow to see if I can get some parts to fix my car."
With the mention of a trip in an automobile to Jasper, Deacon is hit with a barrage of requests.

"Can I go?"

"I haven't been to Jasper forever."

"I can help if the car gets broke."

"If Pap is willing, ya can all ride along with me."

"Pap, can we go with Deacon?"

"I don't see why Deacon would want all the bother? If your Momma doesn't have anything better for you to do, it's fine with me."

The arguing immediately breaks out over who gets to ride up front with Deacon. Mote quickly declares, "I'm the oldest," which has been the rule long as I've been around my brothers. So it's settled. Mote will ride in the front seat with Deacon. The rest of us will squeeze into the small back seat.

"Mote, Granddad and Uncle Fletch need some help yonder at Earnest Chapel. You're the oldest. So, you being the oldest means you'll be going to Granddad's today."

Pap's announcement has my innards jumping up and down with joy. While Mote is fussing about heading to Earnest Chapel, I'm delighted. I will ride in the front seat of Deacon's Chevrolet.

Deacon tries to sooth Mote's pain, "Ya can ride part way to Jasper. I'll drop ya off at Granddad's on the way to Jasper."

That's good news for me. At least I'll get to ride in the front seat for part of the trip into Jasper.

"Deacon, you sure can drive good."

The trees flash by, and rocks bang against the fenders as we roar along the hardscrabble road leading to Jasper. When we arrive at Granddad's, Mote eases out of the roadster as if he's heading to his own funeral. I immediately take up my rightful position in the front seat. Our trip into the county seat is a quick one.

"Yep. I got six fine automobiles out yonder. You're welcome to wander around. See if any catch your eye."

The mechanic, who also owns the local garage, is happy to hear of Deacon's interest in any cars he might have for sale. The man is slight, like an adolescent boy. Heavy black oil stains his hands, and arms. There is oil on his forehead. He wears blue coveralls, which like his hands display large deposits of black oil, and grease. His voice is mellow. Yet, his words come fast, like the rat-a-tat-tat of a machine gun. His prattle leaves little chance for questions.

"Thank ya."

Deacon leads us around the back of the large, wooden garage. The garage, with four large bays, appears to tilt to one side as if leaning into the wind. The six automobiles are a miserable lot. One of the automobiles is a truck. Three of the cars have no tires. Grass grows knee high through the floor of a Tin Lizzy.

The truck catches Deacon's eye. "It's a Roadster Delivery." Upon inspection we find that the truck has no seat. A small crate now sits where the seat belonged. There are also no headlights, and the front of the Chevrolet looks like Grandpa's accordion.

Deacon lifts the crinkled, front bonnet. It's apparent that the only way this truck will move is coasting down hill. Someone has stripped all the wires from the engine. Holes appear where bolts had once been mounted. Whatever the bolts had secured is missing along with the bolts. The engine is coated in orange rust.

"Lookie there." Jesse, looking like he just swallowed castor oil, is pointing at what appears to be bloodstains on the fragmented windshield. There are more stains on the flood of the truck and on the steering wheel.

"The roof will fit my Roadster, and I need the radiator cap. Maybe the fenders will fit along with the running board?"

"Boy, I can't be selling only part of my cars. What can I do with a truck with missing parts?"

I can see that the garage mechanic is a tough businessman. Despite Deacon's plea to buy only the parts he needs for fixing his Roadster, the mechanic refuses to budge. He wants five dollars for the Chevrolet truck. The deal is made for four dollars when Deacon reminds the owner that the truck engine is missing vital parts.

With some help from the mechanic, we are able to push the Roadster Delivery truck out to the road. The mechanic, and Deacon's four dollars, quickly vanishes into the garage.

"How we gonna get that broken down truck back to the Valley?' The question seems to be on Tut's mind as well as mine.
"Tut, go look in the back of my Roadster. There should be some rope."

Tut is only gone a few seconds when he returns with a large coil of rope. The rope is pert near thick as bat handle. Deacon secures one end of the heavy rope to the rear of his Roadster. The other then is tied to the broken down truck.

"Looks like you're gonna learn how to drive today."

"Me?" Deacon is looking at me.

"Yep, you're the next oldest."

"I ain't ever sat in the front seat but two times. How do you expect me to drive?"

"Just hold the wheel steady. Keep the truck in my tire tracks."

"I don't think this is good such a good idea."

"Are you gonna drive a pair of mules all your life?"
"Ain't ever driven a team of mules either."

"You gotta do this. It's the only way I can get that truck back to the Valley."

"It's your four dollars."

With a dirty rag I discovered, I wet it and wash the bloodstains off the steering wheel. Then, Jesse joins me in the truck. He stands next to opposite door appearing as if he's ready to jump out if I allow the truck to wander too far from the road.

Deacon shows me how he has set the truck's gears in neutral, allowing his Roadster to pull the truck, leaving me only to deal with the steering wheel. My armpits are leaking. I feel sweat rolling down my side.

Deacon is in his Roadster while I'm sitting on the box in the tethered truck watching the Roadster slowly pull away. Suddenly I feel a tug, like a big catfish on the end of the fishing line. The truck is moving. It's a struggle to keep the truck in the tracks of Deacon's Roadster. My wrestling match with the steering intensifies as the wobbling increases. Deacon continues to accelerate. My arms, shoulders, and upper body shake as I fight to keep the truck on the road.

Deacon's route to get us out of Jasper seems willy-nilly as we wind through the streets, leaning at corners, and dodging people and dogs that wander into the road. My knuckles are turning white as I squeeze the steering wheel.

"Yeow."Nitwit and lunkhead is what I'm thinking of Deacon when suddenly the door of a shiny Ford Delux opens in my path. Deacon had already passed by the Ford. The truck is headed for the door that's blocking our path like a soaring hawk bearing down on an unsuspecting creature.

Crash. Thud. Crunch. The truck's fender catches the door of the Ford, tearing it from it's hinges. I feel my stomach knot up, and sweat is dripping from my head and upper lip. I immediately think of the police, jail, and Momma having to visit me in jail.

I turn to look at the door as it flips and twists in the road. A man wearing a fancy suit explodes from the severely damaged sedan. Jesse like a possum stands motionless, watching the scene unfold behind us.

"What's he doing?"

"Jumping up and down. Shaking his fist. He's picking up rocks. He's throwing'em at us. Ain't you gonna stop?"

"Can't unless Deacon stops. Besides, I don't think the brakes work too good."

Jesse and I travel on in silence. The only sounds are the wind blowing through the broken windshield, the rattle of the now mangled fender, and my heart pounding.

"What happened to the fender?" Deacon blurts when we roll to a stop in Oakman.

Before I can respond Jesse pops off, "We had a crash. Took the door right of some fella's Ford."

"What? How? Why didn't you stop?"

"How was I suppose to stop with you pulling me down the road?"

"Recognize the man?"

"Never laid eyes on him until he was standing in the road."

"Let me think on this a spell. We need to tell Pap."

"I might as well cut a switch soon as we get home."

"My fault much as yours. If Pap decides that a licking is needed, it'll be me."

We crawl back into the automobiles, and resume our homeward trek. As soon we arrive home, Deacon tells Pap of the mess we've created in Jasper.

Pap doesn't speak for some time, then says, "You boys got church tomorrow. School the next day. Next Saturday we'll drive into Jasper. We'll look up that fellow, and his Ford. We'll fix things right with him."

Amen. Pap's going back to Jasper with us. I sure wasn't looking forward to meeting that fella all my lonesome.

———

Chapter 5
A Cold December

Come Sunday there is no sign of the Ford Deluxe, or the driver. We've spent an entire Saturday walking the streets of Jasper, asking shopkeepers and everyone we encounter, if they know the owner of the Ford sedan. Deacon returned to the garage where he'd purchased the broken down truck, but the mechanic was of no help. We've struck out, no one knows anything about the man, or any Ford with a missing door.

My feet ache. The cardboard I had inserted into my old boots offers neither support, nor protection from the cold. We're sitting on the running board of Deacon's Chevrolet, which is parked next to the Telephone Exchange. We're plotting our next move when a lady dashes out of the Exchange as if her hair's on fire. Her eyeglasses are tilted, her arms flapping like a wounded duck. She's hysterical, and raving, "They sunk our boat. They sank a Navy ship."

Like storm clouds gathering, a crowd quickly surrounds the woman.
Some of the local folks attempt to calm her. "Mabel," they plead, "settle down."
The crowd strives to discover the root of her frenzy. "Who sank a ship?" "What ship?" Mabel is bombarded with questions.

We make room so as she can sit on the running boards of Deacon's roadster. The gray haired telephone operator still wears her black earphones over her head, it's black cord dangles over her shoulder. Gasping, her shoulders rapidly rise and fall. She finally catches her breath.

"The Japanese have sunk a Navy ship over in China."

The crowd now fills the sidewalk, and is buzzing with questions and anger. Some of the men are fuming. There are immediate calls for sending a fleet to Japan.

"Pap, ya think Chip could be on that ship that got sunk?"

"Chip's still up north, training at Great Lakes. He's safe today."

The crowd stirs when a large man works his way into our midst. The man wears a white shirt that is stretched so tightly over his large waist it appears that the buttons can pop off at any moment. His tie is loose at the neck. His black trousers are held up with large, black suspenders. The man pushes his way through the crowd, making his way to the disheveled telephone operator. "Her boy's in the Navy." Taking Mabel by the arm he helps her to her feet, and escorts her slowly back into the Exchange.

When there is no other news regarding the Navy ship, nor of the Ford with the missing door, Pap suggests that we start home. "Momma will have supper ready by time we get back."

Deacon drives while Pap shares the front seat. Jesse is sleeping in Pap's lap. I'm folded up behind the seat with Tut and Mote. The warmth of the cab, the hum and vibration of the roadster rocks me to sleep. I'm dreaming of a baseball game. A Japanese pitcher is striking out "Murder's Row."

"Whoa." An excited voice shakes me from my nap. The sudden swaying of the Roadster back and forth across the road alerts me to some danger lurking on the roadway. A white fury has descended upon the road and surrounding hills.

"It's snowing." Mote is yelling and bouncing up and down.

I watch the snow settling on the road. The white blanket is quickly draping the trees. Turning to see the front of the car, the bonnet catches some of the flakes. More snowflakes rush toward the windshield, only to rise up, and disappear over the car's roof. The flakes drift like goose feathers in the wind.

I hear Pap grunt while Deacon inhales as the Roadster is sliding to the right, then to the left. "Think we'd be better off walking."

"We're almost home Pap."

I can see Pap looking at Deacon one minute, and then next he's eyeballing the snow-covered road as Deacon juggles the large steering wheel from side to side each time the rear end of the Roadster begins to slide one way or another. I feel like I'm riding on the tail of a fish as it glides around the lake.

We're passing the ball field wearing a coat that's white as cotton. Three people are dancing around on the field. The snow is falling so fast that the three figures are faceless. Obscured by the snow I can't decide if they are boys or girls. The figures appear like shadows dancing on a wall.

We sway and slide a few more times before arriving home. Deacon pulls up near the fence. Pap breathes a sigh as if he'd been holding his breath. He is obviously pleased to be home. Mote and Tut are already out of the car before I can uncoil my legs.

"Yeow." I'm hardly out of the car when my ear is filled with an icy cold snowball. Laughter erupts all around me. I can't identify the culprit who had fired the well-aimed snowball.

Tilting, and shaking my head, I use a finger to dig the snow from my ear. Pap and my brothers have all retreated into the warm confines of the house. Any expectation I have for revenge will have to wait.

I'm fixing to tear into my brothers, but Momma brings a quick halt to any plans I have for vengeance. "Supper will be ready by the time you do chores and get washed up."

Like warriors fearful of an ambush, my brother's and me constantly look over our shoulder expecting to see a volley of snowballs. We work at our chores in the snowy twilight. Our breath is like smoke coming from Pap's pipe. By the time I help feed the chickens, fetch water and firewood, my cheeks, ears, and toes have as much feeling as watermelon rind. I wash up in the icy water. Then I eagerly return to the warmth of the kitchen where Momma's vegetable soup and cornbread beckons.

My mouth is savoring the final bite of cornbread when the thumping of heavy footsteps announces a visitor on the front porch. A quick knock, and the door flies open.

"Grandpa." The big man's appearance is a surprise. There was no sign of his buggy and horse when we finished chores. It's unlikely he made the trip from Cordova in the snow and darkness. Pap and Momma jump to their feet. Momma is beside herself.

"Daddy, let me fix you a bowl of soup." She dishes up a bowl of the steamy hot vegetables before Grandpa can reply, and makes room for him at the table. For the next half hour, Pap and Deacon entertain Grandpa with the story of my driving through Jasper and our trip home in today's blizzard. For the next half hour, Pap and Deacon entertain Grandpa with the story of my driving through Jasper and our trip home in today's blizzard.

Grandpa tells as how he'd been treating one of the Ary's for impetigo. "You boys stay clear of Tuff Ary for a few days." Grandpa is looking at Momma.

"Gracious. How Tuff come by that nasty infection?"
"A boy being a boy. That's enough about my doctoring. You boys go fetch the dishpan from the front porch. Got a treat for you tonight."

In no time we're back in the house with the large pan. The pan holds two tin cans, and a small bag. The cans contain sweet milk. The brown bag is filled with sugar. The pan is also full of snow.

"Thought you boys would enjoy some "snow cream." I've never had snow cream, but it sure sounds like a swell treat.

Momma has us set the pan of snow on the table. She adds the sugar while Pap pries the can of sweet milk open. Next, Momma pours the milk into the pan of snow and sugar, and then using her large wooden spoon, she stirs the ingredients into a thick, soupy mixture, much like pudding. With spoons in hand, we dip into the cold creamy treat.

"Yum." Tut's appraisal sums up Grandpa's latest gift.

While my brothers and I enjoy snow cream, Pap and Grandpa talk of the Navy ship sunk in China. "Why would the Japanese sink our Navy's ship?"

"Maybe a mistake, or maybe intentional. Either way it's a message."

"What kind of message?"
"A message for FDR to get ready for war."
"Lordy, haven't folks learned enough from the last war?"

Momma's words are filled with frustration, and dismay. "Let's not talk of war tonight."

After a few spoonful's of snow cream Grandpa eases to his feet.
"It's getting late. I guess I'd better head over to Cullie's. He and Vera will be sending out a search party for me if I don't show up soon."

"Thanks for the snow cream Grandpa."

"My pleasure."

"You best be here for breakfast if you favor good biscuits."

We stand on the porch, and watch Grandpa walk down the road. The snow is swirling around him.

Grandpa's departure leads Pap to remind us that it's time for bed. Once washed up and in bed, we burrow deep beneath the homemade quilts. We whisper about Grandpa's visit.

"It was delicious," Tut's gushes over the snow cream.

"Really think there will be another war?"

Mote is quiet as he gives my question some serious thought. "Seems like every war we read of in history class was fought for riches, land, or folks thinking they need to be in control of everybody else. One things for certain, that emperor fella over there, he poked a stick into a hornets nest."

A week has passed, and Deacon has returned. Using salvaged parts from the dilapidated truck, he sets to fixing his Roadster.

Mr. Earnest arranged for Deacon to use the Company garage for the task. Home from school, Mote and I spend one afternoon salvaging parts from the truck. Deacon pays us a dollar as we work by the light of a lantern. So far he's replaced the damaged fender, the running board, and the shredded roof on his Roadster. One of the dented doors and the bullet riddled rear lid remain a part of the Roadster: a little reminder of the Chevrolet's action packed life. A shiny cap now graces the radiator. Mote said the radiator cap reminds him of Amelia Earhart wearing her pilot's cap.

The dollar we made working for Deacon will come in handy as Christmas is just around the corner. Images of Angels, Santa Claus, and pictures of baby Jesus hang in the windows of the Valley school, the Commissary, and the high school. Momma has been humming "Silent Night" for a week as she works around the kitchen. Tut and Jesse, along with either Pud, or cousin Lynn have been camped around the big stove for hours with the latest Sears catalogue. They've been playing "My Page".

Mote and I agree that the dollar we earn working for Deacon will be used to purchase Christmas gifts for Momma and Pap. We are on the same page when it comes to Momma's gift. At the Commissary we find matching hair clips with white and yellow daisy's mounted at the top of the stem. They will look grand in Momma's long black hair. However, what to buy Pap leaves us with a difference of opinion. I argue for a new pipe. "I like the smell of smoke from Pap's pipe."

Mote is determined that a big shoe shine brush with long soft bristles set on a wood handle is better suited for a Christmas gift. Mote's notorious grin flashes when I finally agree to the shoeshine brush. With Uncle Cullie's assistance, we wrap the two gifts before heading home.

Mote has been sneaking away to the Berl's every afternoon. His explanation for the clandestine activity is, "It's a secret." Tomorrow is Christmas.

Christmas Eve night finds an aroma of baked pecan pie, and the smell of a pine tree seeping through the house. Before turning in for the night I take another look around the room. Momma is rocking in her favorite chair. Jesse's curled up in her lap. My little brother is asleep.

Pages from the "Morning Eagle" newspaper serve as wrapping paper for the gifts that Mote and I purchased for Momma and Pap. Our packages lie, along with several others, beneath the small pine tree.Pap found the tree in a hollow while branch hunting for squirrels. The star Deacon fashioned for Momma, a few years ago, sits atop the tree. Tut is proud as punch, as it's been his turn to put the star on top of the tree.

Six old stockings are hanging above the stove. Momma insists that a stocking be hung for each of her boys, regardless if Chip was off serving in the Navy. The fact that there weren't many packages under the tree is not unusual. I've learned not to expect too much, and be thankful for what I might find come Christmas morning. I fall asleep listening to "Silent Night" filter through the wall. I still love listening to Momma sing.

Christmas morning I position myself next to Momma in church where I can enjoy the sound of her voice. "Peace on Earth" is the Christmas sermon.
"Amen," Momma replies when the preacher ask that we pray not only for peace on Christmas, but also for peace in Spain and China.

No sooner have we returned home from the Christmas service than Mote announces that he as to run over to the Nelson's. My brother is out of sight before anyone can question his reasoning for intruding on the Nelson's on Christmas day.

Momma has set out oatmeal and biscuits sprinkled with sugar for our breakfast. When Mote returns his behavior is like a smuggler wading ashore. Cradled in his arms like a football is a sack that appears to hold a box. Mote slips the package under the tree before he joins us at the table. He ignores my questioning expression. Pap say's Grace.

Eager to get to the business of Christmas, little time is afforded to talking. Mote attacks his bowl; the oatmeal is gone in the blink of an eye.

We help Momma clean up the plates before snatching the last of the sugarcoated biscuits. Pap has retired to the back porch where he is apparently lighting up his pipe for a quick smoke. The kitchen chores are finished when Pap returns to the house.

"Holy smoke."

Pap is totting a box so big it takes both arms. It's as big as the apple boxes that Uncle Cullie has down at the Commissary. Once he places the box down next to the tree, we fall upon the mysterious package like vultures. I can read black writing on the cardboard box. The box is addressed to Pap, and the upper left corner reveals a Navy address.

"It's from Chip."
"Yep. Mister Hanby dropped it by last week when you boys were in school."

"Pap, can we open it now?"

Teasing, Pop suggests that we open the other gifts first. The idea is met with moans, and pleading. Pap, enjoying his joshing, finally retrieves his pocketknife from his trousers. With a quick flip of the blade, he slices the lid open, throwing the two flaps aside. My eyes immediately fall upon a baseball glove. My name is written on a piece of paper, stuck under the strap. I'm frozen at the sight of the glove.

We fall back as Pap begins to pull various packages from the box.
Sensing my excitement he pulls the glove from the box before extending it into my eager hands. I marvel at the shiny, brown, leather. The name Al Simmons appears on the side of the glove's pocket. The strap is fastened with a brass button. A small tag, stitched to the strap reads "TruGlove." A web made of leather cords and a heavy leather strap binds the thumb and first finger together. I put the glove to my face. The glove smells of oil, blended with sweat and shoe leather. The smell fills my nostrils. I love it.

I slide my fingers into the glove. The glove is supple. I pound the leather pocket. The pocket quickly takes the shape of my fist. Pulling my hand from the glove, the piece of paper that had been folded under the strap again catches my attention. I unfold the small sheet. Chip has written a message to me; 'Sailor from New Jersey talked a better game of poker than he played. He bet his ball glove he could bluff a boy from Alabama. Don't tell Momma I was gambling. Your good looking brother, Chip.'

"What does your brother have to say?"

"Just wishing everyone a Merry Christmas."

Along with the baseball glove, the cardboard box holds treasures for the rest of the family. Mote finds a book containing pictures of famous Navy ships. There are marbles for Tut, a car for Jesse, a sewing kit for Momma, and a new pipe for Pap.

"Good Heavens," he must have spent every penny he's earned since he joined the Navy. Why that ball glove must have run him three dollars?"

Momma and Pap have yet to open the gifts that Mote and I purchased. Reaching under the tree, Pap retrieves the small package for Momma.

Her eyes sparkled as they fall upon the hair clips. "Why my hair will be looking nice as Tallulah's. Thank you boys." I knew we had done well for Momma.

Pap takes one look at the shoeshine brush. "I reckon that this brush can shine my shoes and my head too." He rubs his thinning scalp with a laugh.

"Wait Pap, there's more." Mote inches behind the tree when he had concealed the mysterious package he had smuggled into the house. "It's a shoeshine box."

"Yes sir. It sure is."

Pap's gift is the reason Mote disappeared every afternoon for the past few weeks. He'd made Pap a shoeshine box. It's a fine looking box made of pine. The sides of the box are smooth. Each end is shaped like the letter "A." Mote burned Pap's initials, L.O.P., into the side of the box. A wide handle extends from end to end on top of the "A." A small piece of wood, set to hold the heel of a shoe, rests a few inches from one end of the handle. Mote sure has a way with tools, and making things from wood. It's no surprise when Pap's new shoeshine brush fits easily into the box.

We're admiring Mote's workmanship when we hear an automobile pulling up in front of the house. I recognize the purring, and chugging sound of the Chevrolet. Deacon has driven over from Sipsey for Christmas. The family gathers on the front porch as my oldest brother emerges from the Roadster. Deacon, looking more and more like Pap everyday, is dressed in brown trousers, a white shirt, and a new fedora.

Tut's excited to see our oldest brother. "Deacon brought presents too."

Deacon is carrying two cardboard boxes. Tut rushes to ease Deacon of his holiday burden.

Once inside the house, little time is wasted. We dive into the boxes that Deacon has carried home. We're like pirates who've just discovered buried treasure as we peer into a box filled with Cracker Jacks, Goo Goo Clusters, and Moon Pies. There is also a spool of bright red ribbon for Momma, and a set of Dominos for Pap. It's a grand Christmas morning for sure.

With the last of the gifts open, Pap corrals Deacon for a game of Dominos. I have to pull Mote and Tut away from the treasure chest of sweets. Despite the cold that surrounds the house, I'm eager to break in my new ball glove. Grudgingly the two consent to a game of Annie, Annie Over. In no time Conky and Sandler join us. Hustling to get under every thrown ball, as it appears over the house, I grow more comfortable with my ball glove. It feels like it had been molded for my hand. Wearing heavy jackets, we pass the morning playing until Momma calls us in for Christmas supper. It's no surprise that Sadler and the Jones family share Momma's Christmas cooking.

The Christmas meal of chicken, rutabagas, cornbread, canned Black Eyed peas, and pecan pie leaves me feeling as if my over-alls are set to bust. Feeling bloated, I'm none to eager for any more ball playing.

Deacon is set for his trip back over to Sipsey when he declares there is one more package out in the Chevrolet. He quickly dispatches Mote and Tut to bring it up to the porch. The package is wrapped in heavy brown paper. The size, and weight, of the package demands every bit of muscle that my brothers can muster.

Tripping and straining they finally heft the load onto the porch. Deacon urges Tut to remove the heavy shop paper. As Tut rips the paper free I recognize the rust stained door that had been mounted on the truck that we retrieved from Jasper. Everyone is quiet, looking at the truck door as if it had grown legs, and walked up on the porch by it's lonesome.

Finally, Mote curiosity is killing him. "Why ya giving us a door for an automobile?"
Deacon is smiling as he looks at me. "It's a reminder."

"What kind of reminder?"

"Should Spike ever get a automobile of his own, you best think twice about riding along with him."

The more I protest, the louder the laughter becomes. Watching and listening to my family and pals laugh, I can't hold back as I start laughing with them. Deacon and I have sure filled this Christmas day with joy and laughter.

The house is dark. A critter is scampering around under the house. Mote is snoring like a teapot just before it burst into a whistle. Those are the only sounds that fill the darkness. Exhausted from a day of Christmas surprises, everyone has surrendered to the peace and comfort of a bed piled high with quilts. Next to me, I sense my brother's breathing. The rhythm signals the end of his day. I ease to the edge of the bed. I feel for the gift that's lying on the floor. I find the TruGlove. I lift it to my face.

For what is probably the hundredth time today, I embrace the fragrance imbedded in the baseball glove. I slide one hand into the glove. With the other hand I rub a fist deep into the fine leather pocket. I envision a deep blue sky. I the feel the outfield grass as I chase down a deep fly ball. Springtime, and baseball can't get here too soon for me. This season will be the best ever.

Chapter 6
Spring Dilemma's

"Mote. You alright?" My brother is flat on his back. His eyes don't blink, but merely stare at the sun filled, blue spring sky. I shake his shoulder.

"Ohhhhhh" Mote eases into a sitting position. With his mouth open, Mote slides his jaw back and forth like the pendulum on the Commissary clock. With one hand he grasps his cheeks and slowly strokes his cheeks and jaw.

"Why didn't ya tell me you were throwing a knuckle ball?

Mote and I had decided to play catch while waiting for baseball practice to begin. Pap has been teaching me how to throw a knuckle ball. My last throw found Mote's big, heavy mitt stabbing at air.

"I didn't figure it'd move that much." I don't know whether to grin or feel bad about the wobbling pitch.

"Why you throwing a knuckle ball anyway? Ain't going to throw one to the cut-off from right field."

"Someday Mule may need a knuckle ball pitcher."

"Huh? Well, next time we play catch and you intend on throwing that crazy floater, let me know so as I can wear my mask."

"Taking a nap before practice?" Berl and Runt have shown up at the ball field. My two pals are standing, bent over, with hands on their knees. They're eyeballing Mote as he sits on the ground, massaging his jaw.

"Look there." Runt is pointing to a lump that is forming on Mote's chin.

In no time Mote is sporting a lump as big as a persimmon.

"Boy, you look like you been fighting and come in second."

"No, my brother thinks he's pitching to Gabby Hartnett. He throws a knuckle ball without telling yours truly what's coming. That ball was dancing left, right, up and down. Shoot it was like trying to catch a butterfly in a RC bottle." Mote, carrying on like he'd been at the battle of Horseshoe Bend, crawls to his feet.

"Honk – Honk. Sounding like a barnyard goose, Mule's Ford pulls up to the ball field.

We, minus Mote, rush over to the managers 34' Ford, and grab bats and balls that Mule keeps buttoned up in the Roadster.

"What ails our catcher?" Mule is casting a weary eye at Mote.

"He didn't know he was catching Cowboy Winford today."

"Oh. Who was throwing?"

Avoiding Mule, I turn, and trot out to play catch with Hop Lawson before our manager has another chance to delve further into who was pitching to Mote.

"Sure as shooting, them boys from Windham Springs will take an extra base every chance they get."

In two days we play Windham Springs.

Mule is sharing his perspective on the Senior team's next opponent. "Any throw missing the cut-off, they'll scoot to the next bag. They'll be taking big turns at first, looking to move to second should there be an over-throw. Balls hit to left field, first baseman best back up second. You outfielders will need to get on your horse and back up second, and third base when there's a play in the infield. Balls hit deep, we're using a double cut. Mule describes to Bud, our shortstop, that he'll be the primary cut on balls to center, and left field. Runt, playing second, will be primary on balls hit to right field.

"If the other guy is the primary, you back him up. No sir, you be in position, and Windham Springs won't be taking any extra bases."

"Mule, what are we going to do about first base? Jack is still in South Carolina. He won't be here for three more weeks. Who's going to handle first base?"

Mote has been worried for the past week when he realized that Chip and Jack had shared first base last summer. Neither is on hand for the Windham Springs game. Mote is convinced that Mule intends to move him to first base, and have Cecil Brannon behind the plate. A rugged coal miner, Cecil has long lanky arms and body. Chip had noted "Cecil's arms are so long, he can tie his shoes without bending over." Being thirty years old, Cecil is the oldest player on the team.

"Cecil will play first base. It's best for his old knees."

"That will please my missus. When I'm done catching, I need horse liniment for the aches and pains. She says I smell like an old horse and turpentine. She's been threatening to have me sleep with the Company mules after a ballgame. "

"Let's get to work."

Like bees leaving a nest, we sprint to our positions in the field. Berl usually pitches, but during practice Mule sends him to the outfield. Mule is convinced that having Berl throw balls from the outfield will strengthen his arm, and will keep his throwing shoulder loose.

Berl is standing next to me in the outfield. We're waiting our turn to field a fly ball while Mule hits one to Johnny Cicero in left field.

"Ya wanna chew?"

I watch Berl open a red and white pouch. Startled, I realize that Berl is offering me tobacco.

"How did you come by chewing tobacco?"
"Found it in my brother's things after his leave was up."
"How much do you use?"

"Shoot, a jaw full, like I'm making a jaw breaker. That works best for me."

"How long have you been chewing?"

"Ever since my brother returned to the Army."

"That was last week."

I look at the red and white pouch. My curiosity is nudging me to take Berl's offer while wondering what will Momma say? Heck, I'll bet all the men in the Valley chew. I poke my fingers into the pouch, pinching a wad of the leafy substance. The tobacco feels like a tree leaf after a rain, or okra before it's cooked.

"Second base," Johnny is yelling to Hop in centerfield where to make his throw. Berl, Johnny, Hop, and me are taking turns running down fly balls, and firing them back to Runt or Bud for the relays. Mule is yelling, telling me where to throw the ball once I've made a catch. I put the wad in my pocket and run down Mule's long fly ball. I return to where Berl is getting ready for a turn. With a thwack from Mule's bat, Berl is off and running. I reach into my pocket and fumble for the wad of tobacco. This is one of the situations that Mr. Montgomery the history teacher at the high school, refers to from time to time, when his lessons deal with a war or battle. Like most of the men teachers Mr. Montgomery is war veteran. When he speaks of battles his mood changes and his voice grows somber as if he's hiding a secret. A secret he prefers to keep.

Now, examining the lump, I recall a word Mr. Montgomery included on our last vocabulary list, "Precipitous." Was this an impulsive act, as Mr. Montgomery had clarified?

"Ya gonna watch it, or chew it?" Berl has retrieved and fired the ball back to the infield.

What a dilemma? Do I run the risk of facing Momma's wrath, or Berl's scorn?
I throw my reluctance aside. I assume a nonchalant posture and squeeze the chaw into my cheek. Immediately my mouth is buzzing. Within seconds a similar sensation arises in my throat. I'm spitting and gasping. In no time, another battle is raging in my stomach. My mind feels as if it's gripped by a small seizure.
"Sure does give the old body cause for concern for a short spell, don't it."

I struggle with the saliva quickly pooling in my mouth. Still, not wanting Berl to sense my growing discomfort, I force a grin. I work the chaw around my mouth. If Berl can chew, so can I.

Willing myself to be gritty, I battle the queasiness. Thankfully, it passes by the time we start batting practice. With my bat in hand, the taste and burning sensation no longer disrupt my focus. I blast several of Mules pitches into the deep reaches of the ball field.

"Momma know your chewing?" We're walking home after practice when Mote takes quick notice of the small lump protruding from my cheek.
"Only been chewing for a short spell."

"How you come to have some chew?"

"Berl's brother left it when his leave was up."

"Berl, you got any chew left?"

Mote digs his fingers into the offered pouch. He examines the red stringy leafs pinched between his fingers.

"You gonna look at it all day, or chew it?"

Mote stuffs the chew into his cheek. His jaw is working double time as he churns the tobacco from one side of his mouth to another. In no time at all, Mote is spitting and swallowing hard.

"What do you think big brother?"

"I could chew tobacco all day." Mote voice is bold, but I suspect that his body is gripped in a mild panic.
"That's gonna be hard to do in school."

Berl, laughing, implies that he'd been chewing in school for the past two weeks.

"Ain't possible. How you spit in class?"

"In some of the classes I sit by the window. I just wait until the teacher isn't looking. Then I just let fly out the open window."

"Sounds like risky business to me."

Just how risky Berl's notion of chewing tobacco in school can be could be tested very quickly. Berl's first class of the day is Reading with Mr. Chamblee. Like Mr. Montgomery, Mr. Chamblee is a war veteran. He's not a big man. Except for Runt and Conky, just about every boy in the school is as tall, or taller than the Reading teacher. His daily appearance reflects his military background. His black hair is combed. His white shirt is stiff from starch, and the knot of his tie is tight and square. His trousers are slick with a stiff pleat. His shoes always shined. He starts the school day with the Pledge of Allegiance, and the Lord's Prayer. I've found him to be a good teacher and I enjoy the books that he has assigned for reading. I don't think I would have read "Call of the Wild," or "Drums Along the Mohawk," if not for Mr. Chamblee. There are only four books for our entire class. Everyone in class takes a turn reading aloud each day. Sometimes I go to Mr. Chamblee's classroom after school to read the next chapter, or again read an exciting episode that we read earlier. Mr. Chamblee is a no-nonsense teacher.

Mote learned the hard way that Mr. Chamblee wasn't one to tolerate sassy behavior. During a lunchtime ball game, Mote had taken exception to the umpiring. My brother thought that the umpire was either making prejudicial calls for the other team, made up of girls, or he didn't know much about baseball. The umpire was Mr. Chamblee. Before the end of the lunch recess, surrounded by both teams, Mote had been the recipient of a good paddling from him. As if the paddling wasn't bad enough, Mr. Chamblee sent a letter home. Mote was to deliver the letter to Pap, and bring it back to school the following day.

Needless to say, Mote was sweating bullets that afternoon. My big brother decided what he considered the best strategy for delivering the letter to Pap. The letter asks Pap to apologize for Mote's conduct at school. Mote met Pap as soon as he came out of the Company bathhouse, figuring that Pap wouldn't take to giving him a switching until he got home. Maybe by the time Pap got home he'd be more likely to dismiss some of the switches.

 "Let's go boy. We can be in Oakman before dark." Pap immediately marches Mote to Oakman, and to the home of Mr. Chamblee.

"What happened when you all got to Oakman?"

Already in bed, my brothers listened to Mote describe the long walk into, and back, from Oakman. "Pap didn't say nearly a word all the way. I wasn't even sure that he intended on having me come home. When we got to Oakman, we went to an area made up of six-room houses. Mr. Chamblee and the other married teachers live in these old houses. Mr. Chamblee must have seen us coming for he's standing on the porch. Pap offers, as he isn't apologizing, as it was me that had been sassy, and I'd be the one apologizing. Pap gives me that "do what's right" stare. I step up to Mr. Chamblee, and tell him, 'I'm sorry that I called ya a cheater, Mr. Chamblee.' Then Pap and Mr. Chamblee shook hands. Walking home, Pap told me that part of growing up was learning how to fight your own battles."

"Pap give you a switching when you got back?"

"No Sir. I asked if I needed to go cut a switch? He said that walking to Oakman, and going to bed without supper was all I needed in the ways of a reminder."

Yet, despite Mote's warning, Berl is determined to chew in school. The best baseball pitcher in the county has a real dilemma. Should he back up his boost to chew in school, and run the risk of being caught. If he's caught he will be facing punishment that will be pure torture.

Berl and I have Mr. Chamblee for our first class of the day. Anxiously I watch Berl as he has a plug nestled in his cheek when he enters the classroom, and takes his seat next to the open window. Mr. Chamblee leads the class in the Lord's Prayer. Between the prayer, and the Pledge of Allegiance, Berl managed to let fly out the open window. Mr. Chamblee doesn't seem to notice Berl's actions. The Reading teacher moves about the classroom. We stand and prepare for the *Pledge of Allegiance.*

"Slam." Mr. Chamblee has closed the window next to Berl's desk.

"Berl Nelson, will you lead the class in *The Pledge of Allegiance,* please." My husky pal has a new dilemma. This situation has all the makings for a disaster. I watch Berl slowly rise to his feet, and idle to the front of the classroom as if heading for the gallows. When he turns to face the class I notice a touch of red saliva oozing from the corner of his mouth.

Berl begins as if he forgotten the words. He gets rolling with "I." The class picks up the verse. No sooner has "to the flag" been cited than Berl rushes to the wastebasket next to Mr. Chamblee's desk, and drops to one knee. Eighteen voices hesitate as Berl unleashes a stream of saliva and a hunk of tobacco into the container.

Mr. Chamblee picks up the Pledge, "Of the United States," and the class regains its momentum, and finishes the Pledge. The class is spell bound. I wait for the axe to fall.

"Berl Nelson, you will march down to the Mr. Gibson's office. You will remain there the rest of the day. You will return here on Saturday and you will wash all the wastebaskets in the high school. When you have finished washing, you will then complete all the assignments given in your classes today. Do you have any questions?"

Berl begins to open his mouth. I know that he's thinking of the Senior team and the game with Winfield. He pauses, and then replies, "No Sir." He picks up his belongings and trudges out of the classroom.

I quickly formulate a line-up for Windham Springs. Eight players. Jack will not be here in time for the game. Berl will be in captivity at the high school. County rules state a team must have eight players before a game can be played. We will have just enough players when we face Windham Springs on Saturday. One thing is for certain, without Berl, we will need to play some great baseball to beat the likes of Windham Springs. How will we adjust to the loss of the best pitcher in the county?

Chapter 7
"Runt & The Little Black Book"

"Ebbett's Field." That's how the Oakman team describes Yellow Creek Field. "Best ball field south of Brooklyn." Yellow Creek Field sets on a ridge south of Oakman. Tall pine trees border the field. The luxurious grass reminds me of the lush, green carpet that surrounds Senator Bankhead's place in Jasper.

There are no bleachers as spectators sit on stumps, or logs. The backstop is made of heavy wire. Benches for the teams are long, grey logs, free of bark. A wide plank hangs between two pine trees deep in centerfield. Signs posted on three trees display the distance from home plate. The first base line extends 301 feet, while in left field it's 407 feet to the trees. The sign in center field is a whooping 477 feet from home plate. The Company has arranged for the game to be played on the Yellow Creek field so as the Windham Springs team would not have to travel so far after dark on the narrow ridge top roads.

 Mule is fit to be tied when he learns of Berl's absence. Our manager refers to Berl's actions as "boneheaded" behavior.

Johnny Cicero quickly begins to warm up with Mote when Mule tells him, "You're pitching today." I know we have a chance with Johnny pitching. His straight pitch is quick to the plate. His drop pitch looks like it rolled off a table.

Hop and I are warming up between the road and the field when Old Reese arrives. His wagon is full of folks from Black Camp. No sooner does Old Reese have his wagon unloaded, and his horse tied to a near-by wild plum tree, than he's skipping around the perimeter of the field

His voice rings "Two for one on the Valley. Two for one on the Valley."

I move deeper into the outfield grass as I stretch the distance between Hop and myself, requiring longer throws.

A sudden pause in Old Reese's cry draws my attention back to the gambler. He has turned his attention to the field, and points a boney black finger in the directions of the field as if counting heads. A look of dismay looms on his face when he discovers only eight Valley players. Now, his forehead is highlighted by a deep frown. His attention shifts between the Senior team, and the Windham Springs Eagles wearing fancy red trimmed white uniforms and black hats.

"Spike." Hop's yell alerts me to his last throw. Hop's pitch has a bead on my forehead. Quickly I bring my Al Simpson glove up. I snag the ball inches from my face. I turn my attention back to the mysterious behavior of Old Reese. He is thumbing through a little black book that he'd pulled from his suit coat pocket. Like a flame on a matchstick, a smile flashes momentarily on the gambler's face, and just as quickly, disappears. Old Reese strides off as if in search of Amelia Earhart.

 Hop agrees that we're warmed-up, so we retrieve our bats and begin to take some practice swings. All the time I watch Old Reese. He has corralled Mule, waving the little black book, and chatting up a storm. It's not long before Mule's head is nodding up and down. An amused smile springs across our manager's face. What are two of the most baseball knowledgeable minds in the county conspiring?'

"You boys gather around." Mule assembles our team. We move away from the growing crowd, and stroll into the outfield. "Listen up. With only eight players we need to take some drastic measures. We are going to adjust our field positions as to who's batting for Windham Springs. These boys played in Parrish last week. We're gonna adjust to how they swung the bats in that game."

I study the huddle of players. I see bewildered looks on everyone's face. I'm not the only one puzzled as to how Mule has come to know so much about Windham Springs. How does he intend to implement this new strategy?

Mule quickly sketches his plan for our shorthanded team. "Every time a batter steps up to the plate ya'all got your eyes on me. For the next five minutes Mule explains his strategy for our eight-man team. When Mule touches his jaw, we move one way, and when he touches an ear, we adjust another way. If he touches his nose, we'll only have two outfielders. Mule believes if the batters see a field open they might try to hit that way. They'll probably pop it up in shallow right. He continues, "They want this game bad. They went out and got two of the best players in Marion County, Bud and Hayden Riley, from over in Guin to join them today. "I figured that Winfield must be paying each of the Riley's five dollars for playing today.

"Fella's, them Eagles will be trying to take advantage of the situation today. Those boys will be thinking too much. They'll try to do things with a bat they've never done. Johnny's drop ball is going to frazzle 'em even more. Millwood, we want three outfielders when one of the Riley's is batting so you move to leftfield. They are line drive hitters so play them boys honest, they're savvy players

I sense a spark of enthusiasm in our team as we trot back toward our log bench. Mule's plan has given us hope. A cry burst across the field, "Hurrah for the Valley." The team is bouncing with excitement. We came to play ball today. "Play Ball." The Eagles are set in the field when Runt steps up to the plate. No sooner has Runt taken his stance than the Windham Springs catcher begins to ride our leadoff hitter. "Lookie here, we got a ringer, they got a midget from the carnival." The pitcher is a kid named McPherson. Mote say's, "He's our kin. Seems like half the Windham Springs squad is made up of McPherson's or Gandy's. Seems like all the McPherson's and Gandy's are all kin to Pap or Momma."

The right handed throwing McPherson has a high leg kick that gives the impression that he's going to fall backwards off the pitching mound. He hides the ball well. Plus, he has a knack of moving his release from spot to spot. It's difficult to track his release.

Runt appears to be struggling with the first three pitches. However, he surprises the Eagles with a bunt down toward first base. Runt and the bunted ball are neck and neck halfway to first. Runt is safe when neither the pitcher, nor first baseman can field the ball in time to catch him. Hop lays down a sacrifice bunt and Runt, never hesitating, scampers all the way to third.

Preparing to bat, two boys about Tut's age catch my attention. They are naked from the waist up and barefoot. They are sitting on the plank in centerfield, holding a large blackboard displaying two large, black, 0's. It's the Yellow Creek scoreboard.

I dig into soft soil surrounding home plate watching for any glove movement by McPherson. There isn't so much as a flinch. He's throwing me a straight pitch. With my arms extended, my bat is knee high when it rockets the ball across the infield. The pitcher jumps attempting to snare it.

The ball neither rises, nor falls, as it flies toward center field. I watch the two scoreboard attendants flinch as the ball explodes into the plank before it ricochets back into centerfield. I pull up at second base while Runt scores. The scoreboard sheets are held up. They read 1 – 0. I'm standing at third after Gus hits a fly ball that is the hauled in near the "417" sign. The Eagle third baseman saves a run when he snatches a drive exploding off Mote's bat for the third out.

The game is tied in the fifth when one of the Riley boys hits Johnny's straight pitch into the pine thicket beyond left field. Still, Mule continues to change our positions like we're on a checkerboard. A slew of pop-ups by the Windham Springs batters are evidence that Mule's strategy is paying dividends. The Eagles are either trying to hit the ball into vacated spots on the field, or are incapable of adjusting to Johnny's drop pitch.

In the sixth, Windham Springs mounts another threat. Hayden Riley, the leadoff batter, drops a Texas Leaguer into left field. Mote makes a diving catch on a failed bunt attempt by the second batter for the first out. The third batter sends Hop to the edge of the pine thicket before he pulls the ball in, sending Riley hustling back to first. Next up is the Eagle catcher. His line drive has me running full tilt to cut-off the ball on the first hop.

"Relay – Relay." With the ball in my glove, I whirl to my left and fire a shot to Runt who's moved out for the relay. I watch Runt take my throw. He then whips around and fires the ball to third where the runner has taken a turn toward home. The batter now seeing Runt's attempt to throw behind the lead runner sets his eyes on second base. The batter is halfway to second when he falls attempting to stop and scamper back to first. Runt pulled a fast one. He bluffed the throw, and has hidden the ball, slick as whistle, in his armpit. Runt runs down and tags the stumbling runner for the third out.

"How you'd like that carnival act?' Runt is laughing as he helps the Eagle catcher back to his feet.

I catch up to Runt near the bench. "Where did you learn that play?"

"Black Barons game last summer. Pap had a Company meeting in Birmingham. He took me along on the train. Got a chance to watch the Black Barons play a team from Memphis. Third baseman, Woods I think? He pulled that play off too."

"Sweet Jesus. You sure had'em fooled."

"Couldn't have picked a better fellow to pull it on neither." Runt's play in the field is the highlight of the game until the last inning.

"Plunk." Runt's nailed in the back with the first pitch. Temper start to flare. Maybe the catcher had set-up inside on purpose.

However, Mule calms us down. "Them boys ain't so foolish as to be throwing at batters when the game is tied." Next, Mule signals for a hit and run play. I like the play, what with Runt's speed. Plus, Hop's been hitting the ball well to right field. The Pirate catcher isn't going to call for an in, or out pitch. He'll want a fast pitch as Runt is a sure threat to steal.

The Windham Springs team isn't a bunch of dummies. No sir. Knowing that Hop hits to the right side, the whole Eagle infield shifts toward first base. The shortstop is almost standing on second base. The third baseman positions himself halfway between second, and third base. "He's going," yells the first baseman. Runt is off and running toward second base soon as the pitcher lifts his front leg. I watch the shortstop move to cover the bag while the second baseman holds his ground.

"Thwack." Hop drills a hard ground ball toward right field. The second baseman has to sprint to his right to shag it down. Bud Riley, the Pirate infielder, makes a great throw off his knees to nail Hop by a step.
"Third, third base." The Windham Springs catcher is having a fit.

Runt, recognizing that the third baseman is still shifted well toward second base, doesn't hesitate, he's around second, and is hightailing it toward third. It's a foot race between Runt and the Eagle's third baseman to the bag. It's not even close. The tag is late.
With Runt at third, a hit, or deep fly ball will send him home. I loft a fly ball to the right fielder. The relay is too late to catch the speedster. We manage only the one run, but when the game is over the Yellow Creek scorekeeper's have posted the 2 -1 score.

Egg sandwiches, sweet tea, and cream cookies have been set out for the after game hospitality. Our ball team is drooling as we scamper around collecting our gloves and bats.
 "Hold your horses." Mule rounds us up, and settles us down on the log bench.
"That was fine baseball today. The base running was first rate. You did a nice job of adjusting to the batters, defending their hitting tendencies."

"Mule how'd you know where the other team was apt to hit the ball?" Mote asks what the whole team is wondering.

"Come over here Reese." Old Reese is standing off to one end of the bench counting nickels and dimes. The gambler nearly swallows his cigar when Mule calls him over to our parley. "Old Reese is the one that had the facts on Windham Springs. He'd seen'um play last week against Parrish. Always keeps notes on every player and team in his black book. Reese would signal me. Then, I'd rotate our fielders according to what Reese had seen last week.

Old Reese is nodding and smiling as the team thanks him for his help. I'm sure that he's smiling because we won and his pockets are, once more, full of nickels and dimes.

I'm sipping sweet tea and watching the wagon loaded with a good share of the Black Camp residents making its way back to Coal Valley. "Hurrah for Valley" blares from the wagon. The team and Mule are smiling. Eight ballplayers and Old Reese's little black book have just defeated one fine Windham Springs team. A team reinforced with two of the best players in Marion County.

Chapter 8
"Jack & A Game For All Seasons"

The dirt on the infield is pitted with thousands of penny-sized craters left behind by the light rain shower that had dampened the county last night. The air is fresh after the soothing rain. Moisture on the grass sparkles like a million tiny diamonds in the sunlight. The Senior team wearing the standard uniform of over-alls and long johns, minus the sleeves, is warming up for practice.

"Ya all just as ugly the last time I laid eyes on ya."

I know the identity of the character hurling insults before I turn to see the newly arrived ballplayer. His face is round like Babe Ruth. He flashes a "Jackie Cooper" like smile. He wears faded over-alls, a white ball cap bearing a red "C," and is barefoot. School is out, and Engine 29 has brought Jack Hauk back for the summer.

In typical Walker County fashion the team falls upon Jack with hearty back slaps, vicious insults, and good-natured joshing about South Carolina baseball. Jack's beloved University had won only five games this spring. I'm glad to see Jack.

Despite the fact that he's only in The Valley during the summer months, he's proven to be a true-blue friend. He never backs away from an adventure, no matter how crazy, or dangerous.In his search for excitement he's taken a few risks swimming, jumping off bridges, and midnight horseback riding, that has left us shaking our heads.

Jack's smile and easy nature are misleading. He stands his ground when fists are flying. He is one tough cookie, even for a boy from South Carolina. Jack has earned the respect of every boy in Coal Valley. He shares his soda and Moon Pie. His word is as a good as if he'd swore on the Bible. He'd never snitch on a pal.

His only shortcoming is his penchant to root for ball teams from New York. When Jack is around, I have a kindred spirit. The debate as to whether Johnny Mize or Lou Gehrig is the best first baseman has raged for the past two summers between Jack and me. Again, that debate will heat up this summer.

The only thing Jack would rather do than talk baseball is to play the game. Jack is a fine ballplayer. His rounded shoulders and limber torso provide little evidence to his sturdy skills with a bat. His tenacity and enthusiasm are contagious. His daring and hustle, when running around the bases, has left many infielders upside down and dirty. His quick hands seldom fail to scoop an errant throw at first base. This boy from South Carolina has never been in a situation where he thought winning was hopeless. With Jack back in the line-up, the season is shaping up to be one to remember.

The arrival of the silky smooth first baseman couldn't have come at a better time as we're set to play Empire come Saturday. Mule describes Empire as a team stockpiled with a ton of former professional players.

Old Reese said a team in the Sally League had farmed out a passel of players to Empire. It's no surprise that Empire has stocked their team with hired guns. The owners of the coal and cotton companies like nothing better than to brag about their ball teams every season. The owners of the Empire Mine are no exception. One Empire player in particular, Johnny Dove, has drawn our attention. Dove has pitched in the Sally as well as for a number of teams in the Texas Association. According to Reese, the mainstay of the Empire pitching staff earns over six dollars a game. Plus, Empire Mine has him earning wages as a truck driver. "That Sally boy got one fine straight pitch."

There is no mistaking Mule's belief that we will face Dove come Saturday. Today, rather than throw batting practice as he usually does, Mule has Berl and Johnny Cicero pitching. I guess Mule figures if we can catch up with Berl and Johnny's straight pitches, then we'll give a good accounting come Saturday when Johnny Dove and Empire visit Coal Valley.

When I take my turn to bat, Berl works hard to keep every pitch on the outside of the plate. He knows how much I savor a pitch on the inside edge. My eyes light up when, on his tenth pitch, he makes a mistake. His aim is off as the ball is whistling toward the inside half of the plate. My hands sting as the ball blast off my bat. I watch the ball as it heads toward the deep right hand corner of the field, making a beeline into the tall persimmon tree that guards the foul line. Dejected at the missed opportunity, I watch leaves float to the ground, ripped free from the ranks of the tree.

Chuckling, Berl waste no time in dismissing the errant blast. "Just a long strike."

Berl manages to keep the next five pitches on the outside half of the plate. So, the best I can manage are four line drives into the outfield. Like a rifle shot, I drill Berl's last pitch so close to the fire balling pitcher that he has to dive, face first, onto the ground to avoid the menacing blast. I'm pleased with myself watching Berl regain his feet and brushing the dirt from his over-alls.

 I can't resist the opportunity to needle my pal, "Only time I'd seen you move that fast is when food is on the table."
"Shoot, the ball would have been lopsided if I let it hit my body."

The heckling, and taunts continue to filter back and forth for the remainder of
the day.
Mule devotes the rest of the day and practice to defense. We play a game of "Race the Ball" as our manager preaches, "Be sure of an out." Mule professes that with Berl and Dove pitching the game is going to be close.

"Runs and hits will be in short supply," Mule's sermon sounds mystical.

The next two nights I fall asleep thinking of Johnny Dove. How much faster is Dove than Berl? Will Dove laugh at the idea of a fifteen-year old boy stepping to the plate against the likes of a professional ball player? I know that if I can hit pitching the likes of Berl, then I can hit most any pitcher. Come morning, Mote and I are still swallowing Momma's biscuits spread with persimmon jam and butter when we trot off to the ball field to join the team for the big game with Empire. "Looky." Mote is pointing at the ball field as we round the corner by the Commissary. A crowd has already begun to settle around the diamond. It will be four hours before the game starts. I study the faces and find a mixture of strangers and locals circling the diamond. The white and green "Birchfield Theaters" van is parked on the road behind the backstop. That Passe fellow is here for the game too. The county is sure fired up about this game between our Valley team and Empire Mine. What a fine day for baseball.

I quickly put on my spikes, roll-up the legs of my over-alls, and adjust my old "Barons" cap. Then I play catch with Jack.

"Beep, Beep, Beep, Beep, Beep." We stop to listen to the noise screaming over the ridgeline, blasting between the houses and buildings. A cloud of dust follows the racket. The Empire ball team appears, loaded in trucks and escorted by a state police car. Apparently every living soul from Empire has ventured across the county for the game.

The entire Coal Valley team is sneaking a peak at the caravan of trucks and wagons crowding the road into town. We watch as the arriving crowd rants, cheers, and rings cow bells.

"Looks like they opened the gates of the asylum for this one." I laugh at Jack's remark as I search the trucks for the Empire ball team, hunting for Dove amongst the green and white clad team. Having never seen the acclaimed pitcher, I give up my futile search. I beckon Jack over, and we retrieve our bats and then swing and bunt against imaginary pitches. With each swing of the bat I visualize a taunting figure of the Empire pitcher releasing a flaming ball in my direction.

"That's Dove." Mote is motioning with his heavy catchers glove to where an Empire player has assumed a pose on the pitchers mound. The green clad pitcher toes the freshly painted white wood board that rests atop the mound. Using his the toe of his spikes, he pushes and moves dirt around as if he's preparing to plant beans. Satisfied with his grooming he reassumes his pose on the mound. Initiating a wind-up, he flings an imaginary ball toward home plate.

"Shoot. Dove ain't much taller than Runt." Mote observation is dead-on. The daunting figure I have imagined is only a couple of inches taller than Runt.

'It ain't the size of the dog in the fight," suggest Bud Millwood who's joined us in taking stock of the visiting team.

Leaving the mound Dove looks in our direction. Taking notice of our appraising stares, the pitcher stops. Dove forms his hand in the shape of a pistol. Then, like Billy the Kid, he proceeds to point his "gun" in our direction, tapping his thumb like the hammer on a six-shooter. He registers a shot at the four of us. With his make-believe gunplay finished, Dove smiles, turns and walks over to the bench, rejoining his Empire teammates.

"Don't think Dove's got much respect for our ball team," grumps Mote.
"Let's see if he pitches better than he shoots," cracks Jack.

"Two for one on the Valley." Old Reese is seeking out unsuspecting candidates who might wish to wager their meager sums on the Empire team. I feel better knowing the gambling trash collector is betting on Coal Valley. Reese doesn't bet unless he thinks it's a sure thing.

"Ain't this a find day for baseball."

The loud speakers roar from the Birchfield Theater van as Passe takes up his role of announcer for today's game. I hear him announce, "Batting fifth, and playing right field," and my name. I sense my stomach flip. My mouth feels dry. I run to right field where I fidget with my glove, first spitting into and then pounding my fist deep into the soft leather pocket.

"Hurrah for Spike."

I look into the large Persimmon tree standing near right field. Tut and his pals are roosting in their usual game day seat, high in the branches of the big tree.

Let's play ball, I'm ready. No sooner had the thought entered my mind than the umpire for today's game cries out "Play Ball."

The umpire wears the uniform of the state police. Mule said the county had asked the state police for an umpire. Several years ago a fight had broken out in a big game. Shots had been fired. The county doesn't want a repeat episode today. The umpire wears a wire, cage like, mask. The state police patch is visible on his shoulder despite the padding he wears like a catcher. He will be behind the catcher, just like the big leaguers. I notice that the umpire stills wears a holster and his large revolver. Doesn't seem likely that he'll get much complaining today.

The county association has done away with the coin flip. This season the visiting team will bat first. When the first three batters fall victim to Berl's pitching, the intensity is notched up around the diamond.

He pitches better than he shoots. Dove is in command of his pitches. Runt had reached first base safely when the Empire team hesitated on his drag bunt. Jack and Johnny both go down on strikes. Gus lines out to left field with me standing on deck.

Berl's second inning performance is a match for the first. It's a scoreless game in the bottom of the second inning when I take my turn at bat.

The Empire catcher is a Gurganus, a distant cousin, who I suspect is as old as Deacon. His heavy beard has a sprinkling of gray, and is barrel chested like Grandpa. The husky catcher immediately attempts to get under my skin.

"Let's see if we can give this fellow a close shave. It's a shame he's too young for whiskers." Dove's first pitch is high and inches off my nose. The Sally Leaguer is trying to rattle me some too. I know the next pitch will be on the outside corner. What feels like a double, and looks like an extra base hit, turns into an out when the left field dashes into the alley between left and center field to make a running, one hand, catch of my line drive. Passe describes the catch "Like a hawk snaring a swallow".

Seven innings pass without either team mastering the pitching of Berl and Dove. In the eighth inning Empire manages to get their leadoff batter on base when he drops a Texas leaguer between Runt and me. The Empire runner then managed to reach second base when we mishandled a pickle situation. Berl pulled the iron out of the fire with some fine pitching.

The bats remained quiet for the bottom of the eighth, and top of the ninth. I'm the first batter in the bottom of the ninth. Like he had done in the first inning, Dove attempts to put his first pitch under my nose. It's inside, but still in the strike zone. I feel the ball buckle on contact. I immediately know it's heading into foul territory. The ball crashes through the Persimmon tree. I watch as Tut and his pal's bail from the tree like fleas from a wet dog. The umpire calls a halt to the game as he laughs at the falling bodies and tree leaves floating to earth. The crowd is also having a good laugh.

I step back up to the plate. Again, the Empire pitcher is giving me that gunfighter grin. Dove's second pitch bears to the inside. Dove must think I'll back away from another inside pitch while he sneaks a strike in on the inside corner. The ball has been left too far out over the plate. I'm rounding first base as I catch sight of the ball soaring over the creek and beyond the tall trees lining the far bank.

The loud speakers on the Birchfield van are telling the crowd, "That balls has just left Walker County." I round third base on a fast trot, headed for home, when I catch a glimpse of Dove throwing his mitt across the diamond as he storms off the field.

"Hurrah for the Valley, Hurrah the Valley," can be heard above all the cheering and yelling.

"There's corn bread, black-eyed peas, fried chicken, and sweet tea for you winners over at the Commissary porch. Come back to the field when you've had your fill." Mule's offer has us sprinting over to the Commissary to join with Coal Valley fans, Empire's team and supporters for the feast.

Admirers from Empire have surrounded Dove when he spots me. Then loud enough for me to hear, he say's, "No school boy will beat me next time."

I join my teammates for the spread that has been laid out by the Company. By the time we finish eating, and head back to the ball diamond, we are a sluggish bunch.

"Ya'all just about gave that one away. Could've wasted some great pitching by Berl." Mule is in no mood for celebrating. "That was a sorry looking run-down if I ever saw one." The botched "pickle" situation has not been forgotten in the wake of our victory. "We're gonna stay here until you can show me you know how to manage a run-down."

The sun had set long ago. Mule has us practicing our "Pickle" defense until sweat covers every inch of my body. A burp leaves a bitter taste in my mouth. My stomach feels as if it's about to erupt with my post-game meal of fried chicken, cornbread, and sweet tea.

When Mule is satisfied that we will execute the crucial run down correctly, he finally calls an end to our post game practice. However, it's not before the dirt between the road and diamond has been the scene of several gut wrenching deposits by various teammates.

Dragging our sorry bodies home, Mote wonders aloud, "I would've swore we won the game today."

Chapter 9
"Quarters for Momma's Jar"

"Sheriff Cox found that baseball you hit over the creek."

Tut's message has me curious as a cat. He ran all the way out to the Bailey Farm, where I'm hoeing a field of baby corn, to share this mysterious news with me. The red soil is warm as it collects between my toes. The straw hat offers little relief from June's blistering sun. The corn's bright green leaves are only knee high, the gold tassels look like long whiskers. The sight of the corn conjures up the savory prospect of fresh corn on the cob. Beside the ten cents I make hoeing for an hour, Mr. Bailey agreed to give me a enough corn ears to fill two sacks come picking time. The sixty days won't go fast enough when it comes to having fresh corn. Ain't anything better than fresh corn on the cob.

I'd seen Tut's friends scampering across the creek, and along the hillside. They had been looking for the ball after the game with Empire. I seek an explanation from Tut.

"Why would Sheriff Cox be interested in that baseball? How do you know he found it?"
"Pud said, 'I saw the sheriff ride his big horse along the creek bank, and then he rode back into the trees. When he got off his horse, he picked it up. He looked around and got back on his horse.' Pud watched the whole thing."

"What he'd do with the baseball?"

"He just tossed it down, kicked some leaves over it, and got back on his horse. Sheriff told Pud he best not touch the ball as it was evidence.

"Evidence. What he'd mean by evidence?" Tut shrugged his shoulders. "Why'd the Sheriff just leave the ball?"

Tut's news of Sheriff Cox's search, and discovery of the homerun ball, puzzles me throughout the sweltering afternoon. Evidence? Isn't evidence used to solve a crime? Had Dove been using some trick to alter the ball? Was something wrong with the baseball? For the rest of the day the mysterious actions of the sheriff, baffles us no end.

When I finish hoeing, the afternoon sun is already deep in the western sky. I head to the ball field where Mote and Jack are playing catch. Mule, along with most of the ball team, hasn't shown up. I recount the story of Sheriff Cox and the baseball. They're bewildered by the Sheriff's behavior too. We are grasping for answers when Mule and our teammates begin to arrive.
"Make it bounce. Make it bounce." Mule has our tongues dragging by the time we wrap up practice. Mule is a strong advocate of the squeeze play. I must have bunted fifty pitches and made the dash from third another fifty times before Mule was satisfied with our execution. When it comes to baseball, Mule says, "There is no substitute for repetitions. "Do it again. Do it again. Once More," seems to be the extent of our manager's vocabulary during practice whether it's fielding, stealing a base, the hit and run, a double steal, or backing-up a play. Mule understands baseball, and how to get the most out of practice. When he calls an end to the rigors of practice, sweat drips off the tip of our noses. Our shirts are drenched inside and out. Streaks of sweat and dirt leave us looking more like gandy dancers rather than a ball team.

Mote and I are heading home to a much-anticipated supper when we are in sight of our house and we spot a large horse standing near the fence surrounding our place.
"That's the sheriff's horse."

No sooner have we noticed the red horse than Cox appears with Pap from around the corner of the house. Cox is wearing his brown fedora hat, and brown trousers. His Company badge, worn on a white shirt, glistens in the late sunlight. His boots are black like coal, and shine even from a distance.

I know Pap had come home from the mine. He's probably been checking on his garden. Tut and I had planted peanuts for Pap back in April. We had poked a hole in the ground with a stick, dropped a seed into the fresh hole, and with our bare feet, shoved dirt back into the hole. Pap has been checking the patch every day hoping to see the formation of yellow flower buds, proof of a good crop.

"That was some poke you had off that Dove fella." The sheriff has mounted by the time we reach the house.
His greetings prompt a smile. "Thank you Mr. Cox." The sheriff rode off without any further discussion of the home run. Nor, why he'd paid a visit to Pap.

"Pap, why'd the Sheriff come to our house?"

"Just wanted to talk baseball." It's apparent that Pap has no intention of sharing his conversation with Cox as he turns and heads off toward his garden.

After supper that evening Pap strolls over to see Uncle Fletch, where they light up their pipes. They'll probably talk about Johnny Vander Meer's pitching, Joe Louis, or FDR's plan to raise the minimum wage to forty cents an hour.

Pap is gone longer than usual this evening. We had washed up and are setting off to bed when Pap finally returned. *"Plink, Plink, Plink,"* followed by a half dozen more plinks, clatters from Momma's money jar. Pap is feeding the jar quarters, one after another.

85

How'd Pap come by so many quarters? Momma is as interested in Pap's newfound riches as my brothers and me. "Good heavens L.O., where'd you come by all that money?"

"Bunch of fella's over at the Commissary didn't think any fifteen year old boy could hit a ball over 450 feet. Said that poke would be out of Rickwood in Birmingham. Me and the other fellas got some twine from your brother. We measured off 400 feet. The Sheriff was there too. He led us right to that baseball. It was 450 feet, plus another 4 long steps. Sheriff estimated 462 feet. Those other fellows felt so foolish. Why they just offered me and Sheriff Cox a bunch of quarters."

Momma's face displays a dubious frown. She returns to her sock mending and muttering, "Never heard of coal miners ever giving away money unless they was betting on some foolishness." Momma must have hit a nerve, because Pap immediately reminds us that we'd best get to bed. I'm sure glad Sheriff Cox found that baseball.

Mote's breathing is like a purring cat. Tut is thrashing around in bed as if he's fighting wildcats in a sack. A light breeze eases through the barren window and between the cracks in the walls. Moonlight beams through the open window. It casts a soft glow in our room. I watch the shadow of the light bulb, hanging by a cord from the ceiling, dance on the wall.

I toss and turn thinking about baseball. I think about today's game. I clinch my hands, and sense the stinging moment when my bat collided with Dove's pitch, and the image of the ball taking flight on its 460-foot long journey. Instead of our field I imagine the ball clearing the wooden, sign cluttered fence of Rickwood. I have the sensation that the game against Empire is only the start of some amazing baseball. My mind races with home runs, squeeze plays, line drives, double plays, and fire-balling pitchers. Can I match that home run against Empire? Who will provide the next exciting play? Will Sipsey, or Parrish field the toughest line-up we face? Surely this summer will be one of exciting baseball.

Chapter 10
"A Season of Firsts"

"Three dollars for playing baseball?" I can't believe what Mule is telling me. "Why does Sipsey want me to play ball with them?"

Practice is over. Mule has pulled Berl and me aside to discuss what the manager of the Sipsey ball team has in mind. "Said they got a big game with Homewood Dairy out of Birmingham. Mr. Earnest said the Company would pay you for playing."
"Why is Sipsey offering Berl more than me?" I know that Berl has been offered five dollars to play for our county rivals.

"I reckon they feel with the Julian boys playing they don't need hitting as much as they need pitching?"

"I'll play." It don't really matter to me one iota. I'd be playing baseball and making three dollars. That sure beat having to scourge chunks of coal for Uncle Cullie or weed the Bailey rhubarb patch for ten cents. The idea of playing with the Julian brothers is intriguing too. Much like the McPherson's, Holley's and Kittles, the Julian's have been a thorn in the side of Valley baseball every season far as I can remember. Now, I'll have a chance to join forces with them against a tough Homewood team. Plus, having Berl on the mound is a comfort. "Could be a heck of a ballgame."

Sheriff Cox never misses a ball game, so Berl and I hitch a ride with him over to Sipsey. We leave Coal Valley before the sun is popping up over the ridge tops. Sheriff Cox amuses us with tales of bootleggers, pool hall hustlers, and baseball as we make the winding trip across Walker County.

The tallest church in the county marks our arrival in Sipsey. The tall wooden chapel stands like a beacon on one end of town. Like Coal Valley, many of the homes in Sipsey are built on a hillside. The front porches are so high a full grown man could walk under the porch while the back of the houses are so low it would be hard to crawl under the porch.

"Jeez, the houses in Sipsey sure look old?" I notice the similarities between the houses in Sipsey, and Coal Valley.

"A coal miner's house looks old the day it was built." Sheriff Cox has seen a heap of mining towns.

The Homewood team is taking practice when we roll up to the Sipsey ball field. The dairy team is filled with players that have what Uncle Cullie calls 'a five o'clock shadow,' yet it isn't even noon. Each player's trouser pockets look to be bulging with packs of Beechnut or Red Man. Every Dairy player is strutting around like a peacock. The Homewood team is a smug, flamboyant bunch. While Sipsey wears the standard county uniform of over-alls, sleeveless shirts, and a wide range of caps, Homewood's uniforms are white as snow with a flashy Homewood in red and blue script embroidered on the jersey. Their red caps bear a large, white "H." They move with tomcat agility and with the confidence of men who know their way around a ball diamond. No question that Homewood is fielding a team of professional ballplayers.

"They got more professional players than the St. Louis Browns."

A fellow with freckles, bushy rust brown eyebrows, and an easy smile, greets us as we crawl from the Company patrol car. Extending a hand, he introduces himself as Buck, Sipsey's manager and one of the Julian's. He points to the field and the visitors from Birmingham. "They cut ballplayers who are playing for teams in the Texas and Southeastern Associations. Hear tell some of Homewood boy's spent the winter playing ball over in Cuba. They got themselves a fine professional club."

"Let's get ya all acquainted with the ball team." We follow Buck over to where members of the Sipsey team are having a game of catch, or batting invisible balls thrown by an imaginary pitcher.

The Sipsey team is made up of Julian's, Coyle's, Campbell's, and Kilgore's. We're introduced to our new teammates. Many of the faces are familiar. I quickly gain a new sense of confidence. The boy's from Sipsey Mine are a tough nut to crack when it comes to baseball and, if there is anything to the stories, fist fighting.

Berl takes up with the Sipsey catcher, a curly haired kid by the name of Kilgore. I know I've seen the name Kilgore written in Momma's family Bible. The younger Julian, John, beckons me over for some catch. After a spell, I join Julian as he seeks out a bat. He begins taking some quick, snappy swings. I find a bat that feels like one of Pap's, and then begin to limber up my swing. I approach Julian when I see that he's no longer swinging his bat.

"Aren't gonna be stirring up a hornets nest today am I?"

"How ya figure?"

"Well seems like if I'm playing for Sipsey, then somebody that would be playing, ain't."

"Isn't anything to fret. We lost a fellow, broke his leg sliding into second last week. Whole team agreed that you and Nelson are the two players we wanted to have on the team when Homewood came over from Birmingham."

"I'll give it my best shot."

"The team knows you will. Locals says you play the game the way it's meant to be played: Hitting, hustling, and humble."

After a spirited practice on the diamond, the game is under way. It's not long before I realize how well the Sipsey boys can play. The second Homewood batter hits a bullet down the third base line. The ball is a sizzler as it passes over the base. Most times such a hit would be a sure double. Not today. Johnny Julian dives for the smoking ball and snares it behind the bag. Then, he pivots and from one knee throws to first base. His throw beats the Homewood batter by a step. This is going to be one fine day for baseball.

The ball moves like a butterfly with hiccups. I think my eyes are deceiving me as I watch the first Sipsey batters go down one, two, three the previous inning. Now facing the Homewood pitcher for the first time, I watch with admiration as the ball performs a variety of gyrations on its path toward home.

"Strike."

Taking that first strike is something I don't do often. Today, I decide to lay-off that first pitch just to watch it's swaying motion.

The Homewood pitcher is a big chested ballplayer. His facial expressions remind me of the actor, Karloff, who played the mummy in the "Mummy" movie. He will throw that pitch again. Unlike other pitchers, this Homewood boy has a pitch that can move into and away from the plate with constant regularity. The second pitch is a, "Ball." I line the third pitch into right field. I trot into second base with a double.

Dust fills my nose and eyes when I slide into third base. The catcher, like the batters, failed to handle the ball's antics on the first pitch. On the third pitch Buck slaps the ball over the infield and into right field for a base hit. I score.

The score is 1 – 0 when I trot to the outfield to start the next inning. From my position in right field, I watch Berl take command of the game. The best Homewood boys can do is ground balls to the infield. Julian, over at third, continues to play like a wizard wearing a ball glove, casting spells over any ball hit in his direction.

Sipsey 4, Homewood 3 is the final score. The Julian boys account in one manner, or another, for three of the Sipsey runs. Despite the victory, and the three dollars in my pocket, I miss the "Hurrah for the Valley" cry and having my brother and cousins roosting in the Persimmon tree.

"Spike, where'd you learn to hit like that?" Buck has caught me with a mouth full of fried rutabagas. "Why I swear some of them balls you hit today were so deep in the strike zone, you took it out of the catcher's mitt."

I considered telling the friendly Sipsey manager as how I hit bottle caps, flipped by a pal, with a broom handle. Still, I hesitate sharing Pap's secret to hitting. I know that the next time I see the Sipsey team, I'll be playing for the Valley. No, best not give the Julian boys any tips. Shoot they're already tough to beat.

"I just play a heap of One-Eyed-Cat."
Buck gives me a whimsy look as if telling me, "My Momma didn't raise no fool."

I have eleven quarters in my pocket. I'm munching on chocolate Moon Pie and washing it down with a RC Cola when Berl and I settle back into Sheriff Cox's patrol car for the bumpy and dusty ride back to Coal Valley. As we motor past the church I have new respect for these boys from Sipsey. Can't wait for them to come to the Valley for a game.

The three dollars is the last money I've made playing baseball this summer. Berl earns five dollars most every weekend. He pitches for our team one day. Then, if we don't have a game on Sunday he trots over to pitch for Corona, Dora, or another county team. Pap figures that Berl made more money during the summer than most coal miners.

"Spike, Mote. We got real uniforms, just like the Dodgers." We can hear Runt yelling a mile away. "Ya got to see'um."Our pal is usually cool, calm, and collected. He never gets overly excited about much of anything. However, baseball is one thing that ignites Runt's enthusiasm. Today, he's about to burst with excitement. Runt ran us down at the Bailey Farm where we've been picking pole beans all morning. His exciting news brings our picking to a halt.

"There're white with blue trim and blue numbers. The caps are blue too." Runt delivers the news of our new baseball uniforms as he battles to regain his breath. "That ain't all. We got blue socks too."

With Runt pitching-in, the bean picking is finished in record time. Mr. Bailey has barely offered over the two dimes, and a bag of beans for Momma, when we're busting our tails to the Commissary.

"Don't I look like Dizzy Dean?"

Berl is prancing around on the Commissary porch. The new, white, uniform only validates how broad are the shoulders and chest of the best pitcher in the county.

Half the Senior team is on the Commissary porch, touching and looking at the new uniforms. It's as if they are a mirage, set to disappear as quickly as they've appeared. In an attempt to fit each player, Mule and Mr. Earnest hold jerseys across our shoulders. Coal Valley is lettered in blue across the front of the white uniforms. Uncle Cullie has set up part of the Commissary where we can try on the pants. In no time the whole team is wearing the new uniforms.
Jack, being a fan of any team from New York keeps saying how, "We look like Brooklyn."

No matter. We're excited to have real baseball uniforms.

"Wait till them teams from Jasper, Carbon Hill, and Flat Creek get a gander of these new uniforms. Why I bet they don't even get a hit, or catch a fly ball they'll all be so flabbergasted when they see these uniforms?" Mote gushes as we march as if in a parade, up the road wearing our new baseball uniforms.

Bud Millwood asks the question that had plagued us all afternoon. "Why did Company buy us uniforms?"

Runt provides the answer. "My Pa says the Company wants the folks in the Valley and the team to be something everyone can be proud of. Pa says the owners don't cotton to teams from Parrish, Gorgas, Jasper, and Alabama Power looking better than the Company team."

We can't wait for our next game. The wait won't be long. We play Flat Creek tomorrow.

I toss and turn all night dreaming of playing baseball in a real uniform. I jump out of bed at first light, and along with Mote, devour some oatmeal and with Momma's approval hustle off to the ball field. We are joined by jubilant teammates, bouncing around as if our new uniforms had been sprinkled with a magic potion. Every warm-up throw seems to slice through the air with blazing swiftness. The bats feel lighter and quicker.

Quiet as church mice, the Flat Creek ball team arrives at the field. The sight of the Valley team in gleaming white uniforms leaves the visitors mum. The Valley team is warming up as if the uniforms had transformed us into the Atlanta Crackers. Each throw, pivot, relay, and around the horn is snappy and crisp. "Fancy," is the first words uttered by a Flat Creek player.

With our warm-up complete I catch sight of Mote. He's chatting up a storm with several of the Flat Creek players. Several times I watch Mote pinch the front of his new jersey. He then directs the attention of the Flat Creek players to where Old Reese beckons, "Two for one on the Valley." Looking like they'd just witnessed a miracle the visiting players turn away shaking their heads.

The game is over before it starts. Berl dazzles the Flat Creek team with a battery of pitches. Seldom does a Flat Creek batter make contact. Our pitcher has not allowed a hit, nor walked a batter the entire game. The Valley leads Flat Creek 3 – 0. Only one out stands between a Valley win and a no-hitter for Berl.

A crack of the bat signals that Berl's no-hitter is in jeopardy. The big pitcher slaps at the ball as it whistles past the mound. Runt sprinting to his right dives for the ball as it skims the ground. He has it.

What Runt does next, is pure genius. Realizing that he has no time to stand up, pivot, and throw the ball to Jack at first base, Runt makes an underhand flip to Bud. Like turning a double play on an invisible runner, Bud takes the relay toss and rifles a bullet to Jack for the third out. Berl is the first player to reach Runt and Bud. He grabs them in a bear hug. "What a play."

Long after the Flat Creek team has departed on the sad trip home, the Valley is buzzing about Berl's no hitter, and how Runt and Bud's game ending play was as fine a play one could hope to see.
Lying in bed, Mote's purring brings to mind a question. What was Mote telling those Flat Creek boys about Old Reese, and our new uniforms? "Mote, wake up, wake up."

My gentle attempts to wake Mote are futile. I resort to shaking Mote hard enough that his bones start rattling."Huh, what, what time is it?"

"What you'd say to the Flat Creek boys about our uniforms and Old Reese?"

"Huh? Oh, nothing, can't tell ya. It's a secret strategy."

"What secret strategy?"

"Can't tell. It's secret."

Before I can come up with a new line for interrogating Mote, he's purring again.
I punch his pillow, but the only response is the steady hum of his breathing.

"Why you dressed in your uniform?" I wake up to find Mote, dressed in his baseball uniform. He's squatting on his haunches in front of the mirror that Momma uses when fitting some of the local women for a new dress. Mote is poising as if he's set to catch a game. "We aint' got any game today."

"I'm working on my signals."

"Why you need your uniform to do that?'

"Cause I wear my uniform in a game." Sometimes trying to get a straight answer from Mote is exasperating.

"What was the strategy you used with the Flat Creek boys?" I hope to catch Mote off guard with the question.

"Told you, it's a secret strategy."
"Who's secret? Aw, heck with it."

My homemade pillow, filled with goose down, drills Mote between the shoulder blades. I duck Mote's counter attack as the pillow hits the wall above my head with a loud whap. Mote flees the room before I can reload and launch another attack.

Despite a week of pestering, threatening, and pleading, Mote insists on keeping his mysterious strategy a secret. Inquiries to my pals are met with looks of ignorance as well. On the Fourth of July, we play in Parrish. The Company has scheduled a double-header with Pelham Tractor, and Calumet. With the 4th being a Monday, the Senior team will also play a game on Saturday. On Saturday we play Berry. I give up on Mote's mysterious behavior and switch my attention strictly to playing ball.

"Ain't they a sorry looking bunch?" Our team is feeling sympathy for the Berry team. They arrived wearing over-alls, and sleeveless shirts. Their uniforms look much like our old uniforms.

"Don't judge a horse by its color. Just ask Empire." Mule's words of caution are met with nods of agreement. The memory of the cocky ball team is still fresh in our minds.

He's doing it again. As I play catch with Jack, I see Mote chatting up a storm with one of the Berry players. Once again he's putting that secret strategy to work. With his mission complete Mote rejoins our team, and gives me a reassuring smile as if to say 'The cat's in the bag.'

The game is full of surprises. The umpire is from Berry. Apparently, the manager from Berry would only agree to a game in Coal Valley if the umpire came from Berry. The Berry pitcher is a sidewinding lefty. The first lefty I've seen in a month. Batting from the left side, his pitches look like there are coming from first base.

Mule also has a surprise up his sleeve. Mule has Hop pitching today. With his long legs, Hop appears to be halfway to the plate when he finally lets fly with the ball. Berry's hitters are a day late when trying to hit Hop's offerings.

Berry's sidewinding lefty has managed to stymie any chance I have for blasting a shot over Black Creek. He keeps his pitches low and away when pitching to me. All I've managed is a Can of Corn to the left fielder, and a double into the left – centerfield gap. We're tied 5 -5 with only two innings to play.

Runt reached on a walk, and had stolen second to start our half the inning.

"Yow." Bud Millwood has just beaten out a groundball. However, he is yelping after stumbling over the bag at first.

After examining Bud's ankle, Mule helps the flashy shortstop to our bench.

"I'm good Mule. Dad-gum it, I can play."

Bud's pleading falls on deaf ears as Mule yells,"Conky. You're running for Bud."

"Play Ball." Conky takes over as the base runner.

Mote steps up to the plate, and then drives the first pitch deep into left field. I watch the leftfielder give chase. I'm shocked when I see Conky high tailing it around second. He's bound for third.

"Ooooooh. Dang it."

Deep in the corner of the ballpark the sprinting outfielder has run down Mote's drive.

Runt has tagged up and is racing toward home. Everyone's attention is on Runt as he races the relay by the Berry shortstop. However, my attention is on Conky.

Conky, realizing that the ball has been caught is racing back to first base. His sprint to first must be a figment of my imagination. No sooner is our substitute base runner back on the base than Berry's first baseman is ranting about Conky. Immediately the entire Berry infield, soon joined by their manager, is ganging up and raging like a nest of hornets at the umpire. "He can't do that."

The umpire confesses his ignorance. "I only got two eyes, I can't be watching every base at once."

Mule too, had been watching Runt's score from third. His attention is drawn to the verbal melee-taking place in the middle of the diamond. "Any of you boys know what all the fuss is about?" No one on the Valley team offers any clue as to the cause of the heated argument.

I don't say anything. Yet, I know the reason behind the fiery confrontation. Conky, in a panic rush to get back to first, had taken a shortcut. His path back to first had taken him across the pitcher's mound. He cut the distance from over 100 feet, to less than 75 feet. Only the Berry infielders, and I, are aware of Conky's sly maneuver.

Conky scores when Jack deposits one of the lefty's pitches into the creek. I add another run when my poke splashes into the creek on the next pitch. With a 3 run lead, Hop retires the Berry batters one, two, three. The Valley wins 8 – 5

"Hurrah for the Valley." Old Reese is wandering around the field, collecting his winnings.

With a plate full of food and a cool glass of sweet tea, I sit down on the Commissary steps next to Conky. When we settle down to enjoy the post game supper, the story of Conky's base running feat is circulating through the team. I seize the opportunity to praise my pal. "You maybe the only player I ever see that can tell folks 'I stole first base.'

Sweet tea begins to blast from of Conky's mouth and nose. Once he stops gagging, he starts laughing. Soon the whole team is laughing.

The doubleheader on the 4th of July in Parrish fails to provide any antics such as the one Conky executed on Saturday. We win both games.

It was a grand 4th, especially when Mote revealed the strategy that he kept secret for the past two weeks. He called it "psychology" as he clarified his ploy.

"When them other teams saw our new uniforms, and asked 'how we come by em,' I told them that the richest black man in Alabama bought them. They wanted to know, 'How a black man come by so much money?' I told'em Old Reese had gotten rich betting on the Valley. Thinking Old Reese had gotten rich betting on us, those fellas figured they were playing a team of professional ballplayers. They were beat before the first pitch."

I don't know if Mote's strategy of telling opposing players how we got the new white and blue uniforms worked. However, the Valley won more than we lost and Old Reese got richer during baseball season.

Chapter 11
"Hallelujah"

"You boys best stop the shilly shallying, and head home if you want to see that new baby sister."

"It's a girl?"

Mote, Tut, and I had been hanging around the Commissary once Reverend Graber had let us off the school bus. We're sipping an RC Cola with our pals when Uncle Cullie dropped the news that we have a baby sister waiting at home. As there is still a half a bottle of cola remaining, Conky, Runt, and Berl aren't in any hurry to join us.

Our rush home is met with a roadblock the moment we hit the front gate. Aunt Vera, as has become her custom anytime a baby's born, is waiting for us.

"You boys ain't rampaging into the house. Don't think for a minute that I'll let you disturb your Momma, and that new baby girl. You all sit right here on the porch. When the time comes, you can see your new sister. One at a time."

"It's a girl. Momma says her name is Joy." I hadn't noticed Jesse hanging over the porch railing until Aunt Vera tiptoed back into the house.

"She's precious. That's what Momma told Aunt Vera. She's cute. She's got tiny fingers, and a tiny nose."
As Jesse has been home from school for a spell, Aunt Vera apparently granted our youngest brother the chance to see our baby sister.
"She's got almost as much hair as Pap."

By the time I get a chance to see the baby girl I feel like I'd known her for days. Jesse's accounting of her looks didn't leave much to the imagination. She was just as he'd described her.

As had been the case with Margaret Ruth and Jesse, Aunt Vera and Mrs. Ary hold down the fort while Momma is resting up and getting better acquainted with our new sister, Joy.

I must admit I miss Momma's cooking, but I learned that Aunt Vera and Mrs. Ary both can put some tasty fixins' on the table. Mrs. Ary's pole beans fixed with bacon drippings are scrumptious. I especially like Aunt Vera's cornbread cake. I asked her how she fixed it, but she said it was a secret. However, she did reveal that a pinch of cinnamon and vanilla might be helpful if I ever set about to do the cooking. I guess she figures that it ain't likely to happen.

The two women, once again, are intent upon running our house as if they intend on living here full time. Each imposes a set of rules to her taste. Plus, each dictates a sense of order upon my brothers and me. The two women seem to be in some kind of dual. They don't use pistols or fists, they instead resort to fussing as their weapon of choice. Mrs. Ary will leave with the kitchen set in one manner, no sooner will Aunt Vera arrive then she moves things around to suit herself. This struggle goes on everyday for a week.
Pap devises and carries out a master plan that allows him to escape as soon as one of the two well-intended women arrives on our doorstep. Pap evades the turmoil, claiming he's searching for a bee tree, or has a baseball bat that needs paring. Fact is I know Pap found the bee tree and it's honey cache over two weeks ago. By the time Momma reassumes control of our house Pap has finished so many baseball bats he could've outfit every player in the Cardinal's line-up.

The day Momma walks into the kitchen holding Joy is a relief. Pap is one happy man when he comes home to find Momma back on her feet. A sense of calm settles over the house as if a cease-fire is holding. The two female wardens have returned to manage their homes and families.

No one speaks of it, but there is the haunting memory of Baby Margaret. For the first few weeks it's as if we're holding our breath for Joy. One evening at supper while saying Grace, Pap expresses how each day with the baby was precious. From that day on, everyone was calling Joy Precious. Momma finally has that little girl whose hair she could brush. A little girl that will wear dresses and has a bow in her hair. Momma has a little girl who will delight in having a doll rather than a slingshot or ball glove.

As if things couldn't get any better for Momma, on Sunday Deacon arrives home from Sipsey. He drove over in his Chevrolet to visit Momma and the newest member of the family. Deacon's not alone. Juanita made the wobbling bouncing trip over the hills with him.

Leaving Momma, baby Joy, and Juanita to get better acquainted, Pap, my brothers, and me head down to the Commissary to visit with Uncle Cullie and Aunt Vera. Deacon takes the opportunity to ask, "Pap, ya want to shoot some pool." The idea of Deacon beating Pap in any game is wishful thinking. Deacon sinks one ball on the break, and then watches Pap clear the table. Pap uses Deacon's ten cents to buy a couple of RC's for us to share on the walk home. I ain't ever betting Pap my hard earned money.

When we arrive back at the house, the smell of fried chicken and cornbread meet us the moment we step on the porch. My mouth is drooling. It's the first supper that Momma's cooked since the baby was born, and Mrs. Ary and Aunt Vera had taken control of our kitchen. We'd had a table full of friends and pals that Momma had invited to stay for a meal. However, this is special. It's family. As the meal continues, Pap reveals that he and Momma have received a letter the previous day from Chip. Once the clinking sound of forks and spoons stops, and the black-eyed peas, the chicken, and biscuits have disappeared, Pap reads Chip's letter to the family.

Chip's ship was in a place called Pearl Harbor in Hawaii. Chip describes the water around the island "as blue as an Oakman football jersey." He wrote of palm trees, beaches with sand as white as snow, and pretty girls wearing flowers in their hair. He said anytime they didn't have any duty the crew would go to the beach, swim in the ocean, or lay on the beach. "The Navy sure sounds good to me." Mote is all-ears when Pap read of pretty girls, and the beaches.

Pap continues reading. Chip describes as how at night the streets are full of sailors from battleships, cruisers, and aircraft carriers. He said that some of the pool halls make the pool halls in Jasper look like churches. Chip mentions as how the Navy has a shore patrol, like the Company sheriff, to keep an eye on the sailors and Marines.

That part of Chip's letter doesn't escape Momma. "Doesn't sound like a place to be writing home about."

"Why they need a patrol to keep an eye on the sailors?"

Deacon is quick to answer Tut's question, "So they don't embarrass their mothers."

"How do they embarrass their mothers?"

"By not going to church, or being sassy."

Tut seems satisfied with the answer. He sits quietly as the conversation turns to news of the war in Europe. Plus, Japan's attacks deep into China. The talk of war wipes the smile from Momma's face. Her mood turns dark.

"I asked Juanita to marry me. She said yes."

I've been thinking of Chip when Deacon's announcement catches my attention. My oldest brother is getting married.

"Hallelujah." Pap bolts from his chair, and slaps Deacon on the back.
"The Lord sure does work in mysterious ways."
"What ways you talking about Momma?"

"For a long time, I thought the Good Lord figured I didn't need any girls. Now, I've got two precious girls in my life." All this news is exciting until Deacon announces that the wedding is this summer. Smack dab in the middle of baseball season. I look at Mote who whispers to me in a gloomy tone, "Why that doesn't make sense. Why get married then? Do you think we'll have to miss a game? Shoot, we not the ones getting married?" The look on Mote's face is one of relief when Deacon mentions that the wedding will be in Sipsey. It will be just Deacon, Juanita, and her family at the wedding as Pap can't afford to miss a shift. Plus, Momma and Joy won't be up to traveling so soon.

Hallelujah. Baseball will not be forsaken for a wedding.

Chapter 12
"The Squeeze"

"Ya break as soon as his lead foot comes down. If you wait one second longer they'll have a chance to beat you."

Mule is putting us through the paces as we prepare for a game in Empire. For the thousandth time this week he has us working on bunts and squeeze plays. We've worked hard on bunting. Now, I'm starting to wonder if Mule has some strategy that he isn't sharing with us.

"Make it bounce. Get yourself down to first, just because we're bunting doesn't mean we've got to give them an easy out. Make the fielder hurry. Make him throw off balanced. Don't just give yourself up because it's a bunt." Mule's message to Conky doesn't go unnoticed by the rest of the team.

"Why's Mule so all fired up about bunting? It ain't like our bats been sleeping the past month."

That's what I was thinking when Hop sounded off about the new emphasis that Mule has placed on bunting. I appreciate the art of bunting, especially a good drag bunt. I'd seen Jack striding alongside a ball when he'd executed a drag bunt, racing the ball to first base for a hit. Our bats had exploded against Bankhead and Barney, but we lost to Dora and to TVA.

Dora's pitcher, a boy by the name of Ledbetter, threw screwballs. His pitches dipped and hopped like a bird chasing a bug. Ledbetter left us shaking our heads after that game. For two weeks prior to the rematch with Dora we collected corncobs for Mule.

We broke the corncobs in half, and then soaked them in water for two or three days. The week prior to the next encounter with Ledbetter, Mule had us hitting those corncobs all over the ball field. After practice the field resembled a pigsty as corncobs littered the field from foul line to foul line. When it came time for the second game with Dora, hitting Ledbetters dipsey-doddle pitches was a piece of cake. We split the season with Dora.

After facing Dora we played the TVA team. The TVA pitcher, Machtolff, was a master when it came to throwing. As Old Reese tells it, Machtolff had been offered a contract by Chicago, but said, 'No thank you.' Apparently he makes more money working and pitching for the TVA than he would've made pitching for Chicago. The TVA pitcher held us to six hits.

For the first time in twelve games Jack, Gus, nor I managed anything more than a single. It ended the streak where the three of us had multiple hits for extra bases. The fact that we won't see the TVA team again until next summer leaves me feeling jilted. I know that I can hit the TVA pitcher. I want another shot at TVA's collection of barnstormers.

Still, if I can't have another crack at Machtolff and Dora, I have a date against Empire, and Dove. I've been reminded more than once that Dove aims to dust me off every chance he gets. I've heard the threat so many times I see the Empire pitcher in my sleep.

Anybody tells you that The Valley is a depressing place has never been to Empire. It sure isn't much to look at when it comes to coal towns. Like most mine housing, the houses are ramshackle affairs. For reasons I can't fathom, all the trees along the road in Empire have been cut down. The main street looks as if giant bugs had passed through town, eating every tree, and everything green in their path. Tree stumps dot the roadside.

Deacon says those stumps make for some fancy driving. "Sometimes at night a stump appears to jump out of the darkness smack dab in front of a car. A stump can sneak up on driver when the road is full of flying dust."

Few of the local folks own a car, so most of the stump thumping is people who don't know their way around Empire. Men, who spent too much time behind the pool hall sipping homebrew from a fruit jar, have suffered from encounters with one of the knee busting obstacles as they tottered home.

There is evidence of today's big game everywhere I look. Red, white, and blue bunting, flags, and decorated tables line the road. Children are running through the streets like wild horses. Today, the atmosphere in Empire is bordering on chaos. Mule has resorted to honking and pleading with folks to clear the way for his roadster and the Company truck. Getting to the ballpark is like staggering through a gauntlet.

Most of the team rides in the Company truck driven by Mule's brother, Pie. Empire lies almost in the next county. A heap of Valley residents have hitched a ride on the truck rather than endure a wagon or horseback ride. Tut, Pud, Jesse, and a few of their pals have squeezed into the truck.

"Two for one on the Valley." Even Ol'Reese has squeezed aboard the truck. Already, he's daring the Empire supporters to answer his challenge. Old Reese has started his bidding. "Two for one on the Valley."

The scene around the ballpark appears to be more like a riot or jailbreak. The yelling, catcalling, and antics are on the verge of hysteria. Some of the crowd appears to be sipping more than sweet tea. The mob around the ball field is creeping onto the field.

Sheriff Cox, wearing the badge of a Company lawman, has driven over to Empire with Runt's father and Uncle Cullie. The Sheriff immediately presses the crowd away from the field, giving our team enough space to play catch and warm-up for the game.

If the size of the crowd didn't impress upon me as to the importance of this game, the fact that for the first time, two umpires are fixing to call the game signals just how big this game is in the County standings. I've never played in a game with two umpires.

With that in mind, I'm not startled when Birchfield's white truck, driven by the Passe boy, appears next to the ballpark. Passe will be telling how a player "Hit the cover off that one," or calling a fielding gem "Old sweet tea," between his announcements for the latest Jimmy Stewart or Shirley Temple movie. This game has the makings to be the biggest game in the county this season.

"Pitching for Empire, Johnny Dove."

Passe's, smooth, and exhilarated announcement comes as no surprise. Mule warned us to be prepared for the ex-Sally League thoroughbred.

The idea that Dove will be gunning for me is soon put to rest when the iron man takes the mound for his warm-up pitches. He searches the faces on our bench until he comes to mine. First with a nod in my direction, then he throws a warm-up pitch that's fast and head high. Again, Dove looks and nods, in my direction as if to be saying, 'You've been warned.'

It soon becomes apparent why Mule had us working so hard on bunting for the past week. During the first three innings Mule signals for bunts with every batter we send to the plate. Our manager even has the speedy Runt bunting with two strikes and two out. Dove has been dashing to and fro, retrieving the slow, bouncing ball, then rushing a throw to the Empire first baseman for three innings.

During my first trip to bat, Dove had done as warned. He rifled a pitch that was scorching hot under my chin. His next pitch was just off the far corner. I manage to bunt it down the third base side of the field. Jack reaches second, while Dove's throw to first gets me. Jack later scores when, with a two out lead off of second, he races home when Gus lines a Dove pitch down the third base line. The one run lead holds for six innings until Junior Dunn, Empire's gritty and swift infielder, triples and scores on a fly ball deep to Hop in centerfield to tie the game.

Dove's pitches have kept our bats quiet. Yet, one thing is apparent as the game wears on. Mule's call for consecutive and frequent bunts have worn down the Empire pitcher. His pitches no longer hum as they fly toward home. The sound of a ball striking the catcher's mitt explodes with less authority.

"Breezed him." The voice booms from the white truck. Dove had slipped a low one by me on the first pitch.
Runt is standing at second base. He'd drawn a walk from the tiring Empire veteran then Jack's sacrifice bunt moves Runt to second base. Dove steps off the mound, and is looking at Runt. Then, he turns his attention to me.

"No schoolboy is gonna beat me this time." His declaration is loud. It's filled with animosity. The Empire crowd is cheering as if Dove has declared war.

"Hit it to the bean patch Mr. Spike. Hit it to the bean patch."
Old Reese is aware that a battle is set to commence on the next
pitch.

I know that Dove is set to throw me anything but his straight
pitch. He left one over the middle of the plate when we faced
off in the last game. He remembers that hit.
Dove's pitch looks like a watermelon as it spirals toward
home plate. The red, rotating seams look like railroad tracks.
Dove has thrown an out pitch.

"Crack." The ball feels shattered as I drill it up the middle.

"Whack." The ball ricochets off of Dove's leg and then skitters
past the diving shortstop into left field. Runt stops at third
base while I take a turn at first and then quickly scamper back
to the bag as Dunn fakes a throw in my direction.

The lines on Dove's face are rigid. His jaw is tense and
buckeye hard. His eyes are riveted on me. The warhorse is
favoring his right leg as he strides back to the mound. He
scuffs the dirt with the toe of his shoe as he prepares to launch
the next pitch.

The next seconds are like a blur to me. I watch Dove as he
peeks at me on first, then checks Runt edging off of third. The
Empire pitcher quickly turns, lunges forward, and fires the
ball toward home where Mote waits. My brother crouches, his
shoulders square, his eyes peer over the barrel of the bat. He's
bunting. He's squeezing. I'm busting my tail to second base.

"Squeeze."

Every player on the Empire team is yelling. Infielders and Dove charge Mote's squeeze bunt while Runt is darting from third base. Dove is the first Empire player to reach the dying ball. The stellar pitcher's toss and the catcher's tag is too late as Runt slides across home plate.

"Safe" The score is 2 - 1 when a double play ends our half of the inning.

"Hurrah for the Valley" is answered with a mixed volley of howls, and cheers.

When Empire can't muster a hit in the final inning 2 - 1 is the final score. Our Valley team immediately begins to celebrate the hard won victory with Empire Mine's hot-dogs, pie, and lemonade for everyone to enjoy. The team has won, and I've met the challenge of an intimidating rival.

Only the blinking of fireflies, the soft glow of the lonely light on the Commissary porch, and rays of light cast by the Roadster and truck are visible in the darkness as our small caravan rolls into the Valley.

Old Reese, his voice barking, announces to those sleeping and loud enough to raise the dead that the team is home. From shifting shadows on the Commissary porch and darkened houses bursts whoops and cheers that fill the late night air, incited by a trumpeting "Hurrah for the Valley."

Chapter 13
"One Hard Day"

"Look at the size of that shovel." Berl is dumbfounded by the appearance of Big John.

We are standing along the railroad siding, next to one of two gondolas. Mr. Earnest offered us eight dollars to empty one of the railcars standing on the siding. They are loaded with dingy white sand that's used on the mine tracks, giving the coal trolley traction on the rails. There is so much sand it looks as if someone had dropped a mountain into the cars. Despite the huge task, I'm eager to earn some real money. Dimes and an occasional quarter have been the limit of my earnings since Christmas. Today, I can earn some big money.

We're eyeballing the shovel that Big John has hoisted over his thick black shoulder. I recognize the ash wood handle as one that Pap makes, and Uncle Cullie sells at the Commissary. The dull, gray, scoop is like none I'd ever seen. Why it must have be three feet wide? The metal scoop is rounded on the sides and back. Big John's scoop makes the shovels that Berl and I are leaning on look about the size of Momma's wooden spoon. "Big John where'd you find a shovel like that?"

"Made it myself. Used an old washtub that Mr. Edinburg had in the trash heap." The young husky fellow grins as he describes how he made the big scoop shovel.

"You boys ready to go to work?" Mr. Earnest arrives, wearing his customary suit and tie.
"Spike and Berl, you got one railcar. Big John, you got the other. Come by the Company office when you're finished. I'll settle up with you there." Runt's father heads off to the administration office leaving the three of us to the task at hand.

"Big John, ain't you got any help?"

"No sirrreeee. I figure me and Momma can use the whole eight dollars." I look at Berl with a sense of dismay. I'm sure glad I got my pal to help unload this sand.

Big John climbs up on one of gondolas and onto the pile of sand. I join Berl on the other car. Soon the sand is flying as we add to the remains of a stockpile alongside the tracks. Despite the early morning hour we are sweating by the time we've lofted a dozen scoops over the side of the car.

"How much sand you figure is in this car."
"Pa says cars like this one can haul four tons."

Berl's Pa is a shooter. Shooters, working with explosives, do most of the blasting in and around the mines. Sure, I worry about Pap working in the mine, but having a father doing the blasting is a much bigger concern. I've seen Berl flinch when the sound of an explosion rumbles from one of the mines.

My arms feel like they are no longer part of my body. They have grown so numb they could belong on a statue. I figure Berl and I have been shoveling sand for most part of two hours. I gaze over to the next car, looking for Big John. "Berl," I nod over to the railcar where Big John is working. Sand is flying as if sucked up by a tornado. Only the top of Big John's head and his shovel can be seen. Our waists are still level with the top of the huge railcar.

We take huge gulps from the fruit jars filled with well water that Mr. Earnest had left for us. Then, we return to the hard labor. To my frustration, the pile looks no smaller now than when we first started.

The next time I look over to check on Big John's progress all I see is the flash of the homemade shovel and what looks like a wheelbarrow full of sand flying from the gondola. I soon become lost in the agony, and monotony, of the grueling work.

"Screech."

The rasping sound breaks the rhythm that I've set with my shovel. What is that? No sooner had the sound registered than I realize that it's the shrill sound of metal scraping metal. Berl has also stopped heaving sand over the side of the car. We poke our heads over the side of the railcar. The screeching of Big John's scoop stops.

Big John's head, followed by the rest of his body, his black torso glistening with sweat, appears over the side of the gondola as he crawls over the car's wall. He spies us watching.

"Best get over to Mr. Earnest's office. Need to get my eight dollars home."

We watch Big John, his giant scoop resting on one shoulder, trotting along the tracks. He crosses the road as he hurries in the direction of the Company office.

The sand is still ankle deep when the sun slides in behind the hills. Berl is leaning on his shovel, wiping sweat and sand from his face.
"How long you gonna lean on that shovel? My little brother would 'a been more help."

"Shoot, if you hadn't been in my way, I'd been done before noon time."

The insults fly back and forth. Our shovels flashing like sabers as our pace quickens. After what seems like an eternity, Berl and I throw the last two scoops from the railcar. Then we collapse to our knees.

My teeth feel gritty as I rub my tongue around my mouth. My nose feels like it's packed with sand. I want to rub my eyes as they feel like they're each got a bug trapped under the eyelids. Berl's ears are full of sand. His blond hair is laced with the white grime.

It's dark. The Company office is locked-up for the night. We will have to wait until tomorrow to collect the four dollars owed each of us.

My husky pal heads for home. Rocks clatter off my shovel as I drag it behind me while I stagger toward our house. I sure hope they're some supper leftovers waiting. I stumble to the back of the house to wash up before going inside.

I'm in need of a bath. Yet, my body is sapped of any energy, or enthusiasm, for hauling water and filling the large tub. I strip off the sandy clothes. Then, rather than bathe, I fill a bucket from the well and pour the water over my head. The repeated dousing has me cringing from the cold rivers running down my body. I take up the soap that Momma leaves on the porch and work up lather. The soap and water are agonizing as I wash the broken blisters and torn callouses that rage with a lip biting sensation.

Finally, finished with my spit bath, I shake the sand from my skivvy's and climb back into them. I trudge up the porch to the house leaving my over-alls on the porch railing.

Amen. Bless Momma's heart. I find cold biscuits on the table and a pot of chicken stew simmering on the stove.

The smell of Momma's cooking leaves me light headed. I collapse on to the long the bench.

Momma, hearing the back door open and close, eases into the kitchen. In her arms Momma cradles little Joy. A small foot pokes out between the folds in the blanket.

"Lord of Mercy child. We didn't think we'd ever see you tonight."

"Mr. Earnest had a heap of sand that needed unloaded."

"Best get some food in that body while you're fit to lift a fork."

"Yes Ma'am." Momma and I say Grace.

I finish eating, and then chat with Mote and Pap for a spell. Finally, I trek off to bed.

The light, hanging from the ceiling, cast its yellow glow over the room. Jesse is sleeping in one bed. Tut lies awake on the bed that he shares with Mote. His eyes are glued to the ceiling as if he can see the stars shining over the Valley. My young brother seems unaware of my appearance in the room.

"You learning to sleep with your eyes open?"

"Hi Spike." Tut immediately returns to contemplating the roof over his head.

"Boy, ain't you a live wire tonight."

"I went squirrel hunting with Pap today."

"How ya do?"

"I didn't have a gun, but I had my slingshot. I killed a bird with one flip. Then, Pap asks me if I'm going to eat the bird?"

I said, "I reckon it's too small."

"Pap turned real quiet. Then he says, 'You ever think how quiet and lonely the woods would be if folks killed all the birds?'

I continue to watch Tut as he again turns his eyes to the ceiling. Once more silence fills the room. I snatch the cord dangling from the light bulb, leaving the room pitch black. I crawl into bed. I quickly nod off when I hear Tut's mournful voice.

"Nope, if I can't eat it, then there's no need for killing it."

Tut and me, we've both had a hard day.

Chapter 14
"We'll Show'em"

"Huff, Ugh, Huff, Ugh."

I've thrown my body over Lewis Ary, and Gus Cicero, nearing ten loops in what Coach Gibson calls "monkey rolls." Football season is well into autumn.

Drew Gibson is our coach. When we encounter him around town or at practice we call him "Coach." When we're in the high school he's "Mr. Gibson" as he also serves as the high school principal. Today, as he does everyday when the final bell rings, he hustled out to the football field. He's removed his suit coat, but still wears his white shirt with the sleeves rolled up to the elbow. His tie is thrown over his shoulder and a whistle dangles from a black shoelace around his neck. A Samford University baseball cap shields his thinning hairline. The man's trousers are rolled half way up his calves. He exchanged his shined Oxfords for a pair of cleated football shoes.

We've done so many calisthenics that I can't keep track of them all. Prior to the monkey rolls, we did another of Coach Gibson's favorites, "burpees." After doing those for five minutes the whole team is huffing and stumbling as we try to catch our breath. Sweat cascades from my chin and has drenched my jersey. The sores gained from scooping sand for Mr. Earnest seem like minor irritations compared to football practice.

I don't know who the sorry soul was that introduced these exercises to Coach Gibson, which we've been doing for the past half hour, but I'm sure my Oakman teammates would love to thank that fellow personally.

After about his tenth attempt, Gus finally manages to keep his feet together. He has learned to flip them skyward. He'd been dragging them, and kicking both Lewis and me. I am thrusting my body off the ground, over Gus, and rolling under Lewis, when I hear Coach shout. "Go, Go, Go, Go." It's Coach's signal for us to move on.

We bounce to our feet and sprint off toward one of the dirty white dummies that Coach's assistant, Frank Corry, had set in the middle of the field. One year behind me in school, Frank Corry is a small, quiet kid, with an easygoing personality, and one sharp-cookie. More than once I've heard him called a "good egg" by my pals and classmates. His mother is one of the teachers at the high school. His father is the postmaster in Oakman. When Coach asked Frank to be the manager it was probably due to his ability to carry through on a task and doing things that needed getting done without having to be asked. One player tried bossing Frank around, but Coach would have none of it. That player spent the whole practice running up to the top of the Corry Mine Hill that looms over the field. Frank is Coach's number one assistant.

Lewis beats Gus and me to the dummy fifty yards from where we've been bouncing and rolling over each other for a good share of the day. As a result of Lewis's fast feet, Gus and I now have to run to the far end of the field. We have to get back before it's our turn. Otherwise, we'll have to do burpees until the entire team has completed a round of monkey rolls.

"Dang-gum, my mouth feels like it's stuffed with cotton." Gus only replies with a grunt. His panting is rushed and deep. He sounds like the Dinky engine steaming and chugging as it pulls the coal trolley up to the tipple station.

I try to spit, but only manage to emit thick milky white spittle. My side aches like I've been stabbed.

Last season the high school team finished on a roll, winning five straight games. For me, the highlight came when I entered the game to play tailback in the Parrish game. Coach had me so prepared that my jitters vanished as soon as he slapped me on the shoulder and sent me into the game. By the time I got in the game our seasoned players, lead by Gus Cicero, Fred Barnett, and Johnny Ray Kirkpatrick had put a country licking on the purple and white clad boys from up the road.

This season Coach Gibson inserted me, full time, into the tailback position. I guess it's because I can throw some, and can execute all the plays. Plus, with Berl, Lewis, and Red Ferguson in the backfield, there isn't much need for me to be running with the ball.

Gus, Fred, and Johnny Ray Kirkpatrick have returned to blast lanes into the defense. I realized how good these boys were in an earlier game played after a heavy rain had soaked the field. Gus, Fred, and Johnny Ray were caked with mud all over the front of their blue uniforms. The fellows they were blocking had mud thick as mush on their backside. Those poor fellows facing my teammates spent most of the game looking up at the clouds soaring in the Alabama sky.

Our next game is Saturday against Eldridge. A tie game with Dora has been the only set back for our Wildcats. Still, Coach Gibson reminds us that the next five weeks will be a challenge.

Playing on a Saturday means we'll have a good crowd. The folks that can't make the trip to Tuscaloosa to watch the University play will show up for our game. The people of Walker County turn out for any football game. With some of the teams having played on Friday, the Eldridge game is sure to draw Dora, Jasper, and Carbon Hill fans too.

It's Friday night and I'm fidgeting. The only other football team within walking distance is Parrish, and they play on Saturday as well. There is no World Series on the radio. The Yankees dispatched the Reds in four games thanks to the timely hitting of DiMaggio, Keller, and Dickey. I spend Friday night hanging around the Commissary watching Uncle Rich show some fella's how to shoot pool. The night before a football game can be one of the longest nights of the year.

Come morning of the game it's all I can do to eat the oatmeal that Momma set out. My stomach is flipping and flopping. My lack of appetite hasn't gone unnoticed by Mote.

"If you ain't gonna eat that oatmeal, ya mind if I have it."

Mote hardly waits for my reply as he quickly attacks the bowl I pass over to him.
The fact we have a game today doesn't seem to be of much concern to Mote.

"Ain't you a little nervous about the game?"

"What's to be nervous about? Far as I know Charley Boswell is suiting up for the Crimson Tide today, not for Elderidge?

Mote plays end opposite of Runt. When it comes time for me to throw a pass, Mote will assure me that if I threw him the ball, 'It's a sure fired touchdown.'
My older brother takes pride in Runt's catches. He tells everyone that he's the decoy. 'Every player on the other team is set to pounce on me the moment Spike looks my way.'

 "Sis – Boom – Rah." Dressed in blue sweaters and white skirts, the Oakman cheerleaders yell, jump, and wave their blue and white paper pom-poms as they greet our appearance on the field this afternoon. "Sis – Boom – Rah."

The latest addition to our high school is the girl cheerleaders. The decision to have girls as cheerleaders was met with a hailstorm. 'It would lead to the ladies having masculine features. It was unbecoming of young women to be jumping around and making a spectacle of themselves.' The arguments flew for weeks on end. Only when reminded that the University has female cheerleaders was the debate settled.

My blue jersey with the bold white "98" on the front is stretched tight across my pads. The blue, thick leather helmet with a white forehead pad and three white stripes flaring over the top, squeezes against my ears. I feel like a warrior.

"Sis - Boom- Rah.

Following a good bout of calisthenics, our team turns to tackling. I'm paired up with Berl who attempts to rip my torso from my waist. The butterflies that have been camping in my stomach, pestering me for the past twelve hours, are gone thanks to my pal. I'm excited, but calm. My vision is clear, my warm-up passes are on target, and the hand-offs to my mates in the backfield are sharp. We function with marching band precision. We are ready for Elderidge.

We score on the first series of plays. I receive the center pass from Gus, and with Red as my escort, I sprint for the right flank. The defense is running like a pack of wild dogs when I hand the ball, on what Coach calls "49 Reverse," to Lewis Ary sneaking across from his wingback position. Lewis is a wisp of player that many teams have taken lightly only to learn that if given an opening big enough for a cat to dart through, Lewis will find it. He is so quick he can run through a thundershower and miss every raindrop. Once he has the ball Lewis follows Berl and Johnny Ray around the end of the line where the two stalwarts demolish a host of the Mountaineers.

While Oakman fans cheered and the Elderidge fans wailed in agony our sleek wingback sailed down the sidelines for a score. Our lead is short lived as Elderidge powers it's way to a score before the first quarter is over.

As the game progresses the "Mountaineers" begin throwing up barricades for everything we throw at them. The Elderidge defense plays with a ferocity and confidence that has our team flustered and anxious. The Mountaineers meet every running play we attempt with a host of tacklers. When I attempt to pass, Runt and Mote are saddled with half the Eldridge defense.

"You sure Elderidge is playing with only eleven players?" Mote's question pretty well sums up how we're feeling as we begin our half-time intermission.

"Spike, Spike, Spike, I know how to beat'um." Tut is waiting for me the moment I walk off the field. I ignore his rants. "I know what them other guys are fixing to do when you got the ball."

I push into the body of players heading off the field. I escape my little brother's gestures, and squawking. Frank, the slender team manager, bars Tut from following the team into the school.

The score is 6 – 6 when the second half starts. Led by Berl, Gus, and Mote our defense resembles a wrecking crew. Elderidge is forced to punt after only three plays. Runt catches the Elderidge punt and is snowed under after a short run. The referee calls a stop to the game while an Elderidge player hobbles to the sideline. The game is at a standstill when our team manager rushes onto the field. His bucket is splashing water on his pant leg. A towel is tucked into his belt. Why is Frank dashing onto the field? The second half has just begun.

"Spike. You need to listen to what your brother has to say. It makes sense. He figured out why Elderidge is stopping us cold."

I look at Frank like he's off his rocker. "Listen to what he told me."

"You're licking your thumb when you are setting to pass. Elderidge is packing everyone on the line when you don't lick your thumb, and then corralling Runt and Mote when you do lick'em."

"Tut told you that?" I realize immediately that Tut is on to something. I do lick my thumb when I know I'm setting to throw a pass. I'll have to pull a fast one on the Eldridge boys.

Once we resume play I put Tut's theory to work. I don't resort to any licking before I accept the pass from center. Sure enough, all eleven Mountaineer players are either on the line, or creeping forward. I repeat the performance. Again, the defense is building a wall with all eleven defenders. Fine with me. If they are going to dance, I'm going to make them pay the fiddler.

On the third play I call for a pass play that looks very much like the "49 Reverse" that lead to our early score. The difference is that I won't hand the ball to Lewis. I watch the Elderidge players looking for the tip-off; is he throwing, or running? Seeing that there's no thumb licking, the orange clad defense rallies for an assault against our line.

Once I receive the pass from center, I fake to Lewis running toward the left sideline. I keep the ball, and look for Mote and Runt crossing behind the defense. It's "30 Ends Cross". In addition to the fine stable in the backfield, I'm lucky to have Runt to throw to on occasion. Runt isn't as fast as Lewis, but he can tie knots in your shoelaces with his shakes and jitter bug antics. Twice this season Runt left a defender lying on the ground while racing under one of my passes. Trying to stay with Runt, the defender's feet got tangled trying to match the twists and twirls that Runt performed escaping the defensive player's attention.

I watch Runt, crafty at sneaking down field, allowing Mote to draw the single Mountaineer defender away. He then angles toward the far, deep, corner of the field. Twenty-one players, and half of Walker County, watch as Runt, running alone, takes my pass, and never breaks stride until he is in the end zone.

The final score is 20 – 6. The Mountaineers fell for my ploy one more time. Only this time I licked my thumb, and handed the ball to Berl who's as tough a customer on the football field as he is when he's on the pitching mound. With Lewis and Red in the backfield, stretching the defense from sideline to sideline, Berl will find the soft underbelly of the defenses. If a defender grabs hold of Berl that boy better hope that several teammates gets there pretty quick to help bring Berl down. Least wise, that fellow is sure to be hanging on for dear life.

Against the Mountaineers my pal manages to break several tackles and bruise the pride of two opposing players before he bursts into the clear. He thundered down the middle of the field for 55 yards and the final touchdown of the day.

The happiest person in the Valley after the game is Tut. The Moon Pie I bought for him that afternoon was, as he said, "The best I'd ever tasted."

The taste of the victory over Elderidge didn't last much longer than Tut's Moon Pie. Parrish, who'd been the sorriest team in the county all season, ripped us up one side and down the other. Some folks said it had been a planned ambush from the start. They'd theorized that Parrish had laid low all season, letting us believe they were good for skinning.

Mote said he'd heard that some of the Parrish players were 'borrowed' from over in Fayette County. Plus, some boys were home on leave from the Army. Those fellas decided to join in the game day fracas.

In my mind it didn't matter who Parrish had suited up that day. Parrish had a tornado in the backfield by the name of Brice Martin. Whether he was running over us, or around us, Martin torn through us like a whirlwind through a cornfield.

Tut pretty well summed it up. "Wait til next year. We'll show'em"

Chapter 15
Bananas & A Day to Remember

"Gee whiz it's cold."

Due to the cold snap and the Christmas Holiday, school had been dismissed two days earlier. Today is Christmas Eve. Mote, Tut, our cousin Billy McMillan, and I have been to the Saturday matinee to see "The Adventures of Robin Hood." We scrounged fifteen cents together for one admission. Then, three of us made our way inside using Conky's secret door.

For the umpteenth time, someone grouses about winter nipping at our noses and the cold air penetrating our threadbare coats. The coats are pulled up to our chins and caps are pulled down over our ears.

Our shoes are filled with newspaper, and the soles are lined with cardboard. The shoes are wrapped with fruit jar rubbers. Like turtles, our heads pop in and out of the coats as we seek warmth in between grumbling and jabbering about "Robin Hood."

We are milling around in front of the Commissary when a familiar voice beckons, "You boys ever see a banana?"

Uncle Boyd question brings Tut's lamenting as how 'Robin's merry men could've used a slingshot against the Sheriff' to a standstill. Our curiosity immediately draws us to the Commissary porch where, Billy's father, Uncle Boyd is poking his head out of the double doors of the Company store.

We scramble up the steps filing passed Uncle Boyd. The warmth of the Commissary immediately has my cheeks feeling as if they're being toasted. The booming sound of stomping feet fills the immense Commissary as we strive to shake off the tingling sensation that occupies the spot where we once knew our toes existed.

"Take a gander boys. This is a banana."

The object in Uncle Boyd's hand isn't much longer than an ear of corn and about as big around as Baby Joy's arm. The color reminds me of the Jasmine that grows in the hillside thickets.

"Where'd it come from?"

"Panama."

"Is that in Mississippi?"

"No. It's a heap south of Mississippi."

"How'd the bananas get here?"

"First by boat. Then by train from Mobile."

"I saw Tarzan and his monkey eat one in a movie."

"Ya wanna bite?

We gotta skin it first."

The offer leaves me dubious. Isn't something that needs
skinning always cooked first?
What's it taste like?"

We watch both Uncle Boyd and Uncle Cullie each pinch one
end of a banana. Slowly they pull the soft leather like skin
from the bananas. With the skin peeled our uncles proceed to
break chunks off the bananas. The meat is soft. Grit colored
pulp fills the cob like fruit.

Everyone is soon sampling the mysterious fruit. "It's mushy."

"Feels like watermelon after you chew it for a spell, but it ain't
very juicy."

"What you fixing to do with the skin?"

"Taste good." Billy assessment is met with a consensus from
the group. We enjoy one more lump of the soft fruit.

"How much does a banana cost?

"Five cents. You can buy a pound for fifteen cents."

"How many banana's does it take to make a pound?"

"Four or five."

An idea hits me like a hailstorm when Uncle Cullie disclosed the price of bananas.
Mote, Tut, and I have been wrestling with what to buy Pap and Momma for Christmas.
What a grand surprise this could be for them.

We thank Uncle Boyd and Uncle Cullie for sharing the bananas before we forge our way back into the frigid winter air. I pull Mote and Tut into a quick parley where I share my Christmas idea.

"It cost fifteen cents. We just spent all our money at the theater." Mote's point is well taken. We have to find a way to earn fifteen cents.

"I know where I can get fifteen cents easy like."

"Where you gonna get fifteen cents?"

Despite the skepticism over his claiming to get rich quick, Tut is adamant that he can come up with fifteen cents.

"How do ya plan on getting fifteen cents?"

"Selling catfish to the ladies up on Silk Stocking Road. I can catch'em with my bare hands under the Company bath house."
"There's catfish under the bathhouse?" Mote and I look at each other in amazement.

"Yep. Water draining from the floor is knee deep under there. Don't know how the fish come to be there."

The brutal cold wind is dismissed. We ignore the sight of our own breath as we hustle over to the bathhouse. Resting on pilings, the back half of the block like bathhouse sits five feet off the ground. The wood sidewalk extends across the front of the bathhouse. Mote and I follow Tut to the rear of the building where the back of the bathhouse is high enough that we're able walk beneath it.

Following Tut, we stoop under the massive wood beams. The late afternoon light fades. The smell and gloomy light leaves me the feeling that I've entered a dungeon. Tut, jumping and skipping, leads us over standing pools of water. Small creeks, ankle deep, meander from piling to piling. Tut jumps to a stop. He points to a large pool that is directly under the middle of the bathhouse.

"Jeepers." The catfish hugging the bottom of the washtub size pool must weigh over three pounds. "Catfish that size will be easy to sell."

We exit Tut's little gold mine and call a short meeting. We agree that Tut's enterprise has merit. Yet, with Christmas only a day away we have no time to waste. Braving the inhospitable weather we round up some buckets and set out to snag some fish.

 I'm stunned at Tut's slinking maneuvers. In no time, and despite their evasive behavior, Tut uses his hands to flip four giant catfish from the bathhouse pool. We snag Tut's prizes before they hit the ground. With the fluttering fish in hand we set off for Silk Stocking Road. We have no problem selling the flopping fish. Next, with twenty cents in hand we beat a quick path to the Commissary. Uncle Cullie agrees to keep a pound of bananas for us until tomorrow.

Sunday morning we attend the Christmas service. Momma is still humming "Silent Night" as we exit the church. Immediately Tut, Mote, and I, with Jesse in tow, hustle after Uncle Cullie.

"Where you boys headed off to this morning?"

"It's a Christmas surprise."

Momma and Pap are curious as why we're not eager to get home. "Aren't you boys anxious to see what hiding under the tree?

We scurry home once we have the bananas in hand, leaving the fruit on the porch. The house is filled with the smell of Christmas as Momma has been working on our Christmas supper for two days. Pecan pie and biscuits rest on the table.

Pap fosters an amused look as we slide into the house like puppies wandering into the daylight for the first time. "Don't ever recall you boys being so shy about opening presents."

"It's Christmas Pap. It's time for secrets."

Momma is cradling Joy in her arms when she joins us in the front room. We settle in around Pap and the Christmas tree. With Chip in the Navy, Christmas has yielded some exciting gifts from far off places. This year is no different. Momma receives a yellow and white Hawaiian quilt. Pap got a red and white flowery looking shirt. "Boy, won't I look fancy at church next Sunday." We all agree that Pap will be the best-dressed coal miner in Walker County.

Tut is like a banshee when he finds that Chip has sent him a football. Chip sent Jesse a box full of metal Tootsie Toys. Mote and I get a picture of a beach in Hawaii for the room we share. Plus, we both got three packs of Goudey Baseball Cards.

We immediately begin thumbing through the packs. Being a catcher, Mote wants the Lombardi card. I'm happy with a DiMaggio card. I know I can trade the Yankee player's card for an RC Cola once Jack shows up next summer.

The best surprise brings a sunny smile to Momma's face. We've retrieved the bananas from the porch. She says, "I haven't had a banana since I was Jesse's age."

Pap looks at the bananas and offers as to whether, "Reckon we should hang them on the tree, or eat them?"

No sooner have we finished sharing presents than the clacking sound of Deacon's Chevrolet in the road announces his arrival. Deacon is with his new bride. He and Juanita had snuck off and got married after the 4th of July.

"More presents." Tut is the first one to the door, throwing it open to Deacon, and our new sister-in-law.

"Merry Christmas."

I know that Momma is pleased. The only way Christmas could be better would be having Chip home too. Deacon has brought us a Barons baseball bat. He hadn't wrapped it seeing no sense in trying to hide the obvious.

"Goodness gracious. Bananas." The sight of the bananas has Juanita beaming like it's her wedding day all over again. "Mrs. Powell, I got something that will make this Christmas supper one to remember if we can have those bananas in the kitchen."

For what seems long enough to cook for an army, Momma and Juanita bar us from the kitchen. It's like they're having a secret meeting. The purpose behind banging pots, slamming drawers, and the new smell floating from the kitchen becomes apparent after supper. It's time for sweets. Juanita and Momma have made a banana cream pie. Only an occasional "Yummy" can be heard as the pie disappears piece by piece.

I think the banana cream pie was something to remember as I fall into bed. I'm worn out from the cold weather, the long day, and the good food. I'll bet that New Year's Eve will offer another day to remember.

Chapter 16
White Trash & Haymakers

"How we gonna get to Gin Town?"

Gin Town is some 25 miles, as the crow flies, across the county line. We'd played the Gin Mill baseball team this past summer. Even with Mule driving it had taken us over an hour to get to the Jefferson County village. Mote discovered that the mill town holds a big shindig every New Year's Eve. Dancing has become a new passion with him ever since Runt had gotten a record player for Christmas. He's taken the notion that he is the Valley's Fred Astaire. Momma's not too pleased with Mote's dancing. She say's, "It's just one more way the devil seeks to get a boy in trouble." Mote's got his mind set on dancing in Gin Town come New Year's Eve.

Mote's desire to get to Gin Town heats up when Tut and Billy announce that Mr. Bradford has offered his Durant anytime we need it as long as we have a driver. Mr. Bradford buys a heap of catfish from Tut while Billy entertains Mr. Bradford with a "Yo-Yo." It's the latest gadget to arrive in the Valley. "Walking the Dog," a "Cat's Cradle," and "Around the World" are some of the "Yo-Yo" tricks that Billy uses to fascinate folks.

"No need to look any further for a driver." Mote guarantees' us that he can drive. Mule had let him drive the roadster this past summer when the ball team went to Parrish or Jasper for games.

Mote's enthusiasm for the Gin Town excursion is contagious. Runt and I are raring for the trip across the river. It would be shame not to venture across the county line seeing as how Tut and cousin Billy had already finagled the Durant.

"We' wanna go too."

Mote, or Fancy as the girls now call my Jitterbugging brother, let the cat out of the bag. He'd mentioned the Gin Town trip to Sara Kate, Hazel Ary, and Marionett Lockhart. Sarah Kate and Marionett could pass for sisters with their honey colored hair, wavy curls, and pixie smiles. Marionett has a reputation of being a Tom Boy. Her nose bares proof of her boy like antics. She had broken her nose and chipped a tooth years ago while playing catch with Billy. Fortunately, Aunt Lola did a fine job of setting the nose. The small chip on her front tooth gives her a mischievous look when she smiles. I think Runt is taken with her.

The girls' pleading leads me to thinking that this trip might lead to some serious consequences. Sneaking girls out of town, and across the county line, could be risky business. The idea of the girls traveling to Gin Town is especially ticklish if their fathers get wind of our escapade.

"There is a dance in Oakman. Everyone will think we're at that dance," pleads Hazel.

"Why not?"

You could've knocked me over with a feather when I heard Mote's response. Has he lost his marbles? I can think of three good reasons why not: Mr. Bagwell, Tuff Ary, and Mr. Lockhart come quickly to mind.

Despite my protest, come New Years Eve we're on the road to Gin Town. It's dark when we rendezvous with the girls near the schoolhouse. Sarah, Hazel, and Marionett piled into the backseat with Tut and Billy. I've always enjoyed Mote's sense of adventure. However, this time I feel that we're on the edge of a calamity rather than an adventure.

The black and blue Durant is by no means old. Yet, the Walker County roads have taken a toll on the four-door sedan. The Durant shakes so bad I feel like my teeth are rattling. Like a fly catching frog, the sedan lurches every time Mote changes gears. I hold my breath watching the edge of the road creep closer as my brother navigates the blind curves on the narrow county road.

"We got three hours till the girls need to be back in Oakman."

I pray that Mote's sense of direction and time are better than his driving. We race through Parrish and pass Fruit Jar Junction. Then, we turn south where we'll ferry across the Warrior's Mulberry Fork.

When our adventurous party arrives at the crossing we find the ferry. It's a flatboat that's tied next to a small boat. The boat's black and white paint is peeling and looks like shredded newspaper. A little cabin houses the steering and the gears for the motor. Over the cabin door a sign reads, "Captain Bert." On the front wall of the cabin someone has painted "Fee." Automobile 20 cents, Wagon 5 cents, Horses – Mules 5 cents each. People - 5 cents. Sitting in the cabin is a fellow that might be part bear. Thick black hair covers his arms while heavy eyebrows and mop like hair camouflages his forehead. The hairy Captain uses the boat to power and guide the ferry, back and forth, across the Mulberry.

Our arrival is none too soon. The ferry captain announces that this is his last trip tonight.

"How we suppose to get back to Walker County?"

"Head over to the Copeland Ferry. Old Pete will usually ferry folks after dark for 50 cents."

I quickly assess our funds. It's going to cost us 60 cents for this ferry crossing. Plus, another 50 cents when we head back to Walker County. Tut and Billy aren't likely to have any money and I'm not asking the girls if they have any money to spare. That leaves Mote and me with the problem of paying for our passage on the ferry.

"How much money you carrying?"

Mote pulls a hand from his pocket. I quickly count 72 cents. I dig deep into my over-all pockets. I find the 35 cents Uncle Cullie gave me for the sack of coal I'd rounded up along the tracks.

Things look only a tad-bit better when Tut offers 5 cents to our funds. "It's the extra nickel Mr. Bradford gave me for the catfish."

I declare, "We've got a dollar and twelve cents. Once we pay Captain Bert we'll have 52 cents to see us through the dance and the Copeland ferry ride."

"Good that the doings in Gin Town are free. The Mill is paying for the whole shebang," Mote assures me.

With our money in hand, Captain Bert guides Mote and the Durant onto the ferry. The trip across the Mulberry Fork is smooth. The only sound is the ferry cutting through the black water and the chugging sound of the small boat. Captain Bert makes for a small light beckoning from the far bank where he nudges up to wood ramp leading off the ferry. We follow the ramp up to the road. In no time Mote has the Durant sputtering along the ruts leading to Gin Town.

"Look it all the cars." Hazel acts as if she'd never been out of Walker County.

Finding the Gin Town shindig is easy as pie as ten automobiles, a heap of trucks, and more wagons than I can count surround the site of the New Year's Eve celebration. The gin mill party is being held in what appears to be a grange hall. Moonlight ambles through the leaves of a pine oak. The ancient tree guards one side of the hall. Its limbs are as thick as a man. A light mounted on the porch roof emits a mellow glow in front of the building.

The wide rickety hall is mounted on bricks so high enough that a small child can walk underneath. The hall's white facing has surrendered to Mother Nature. The only evidence of the white coat is on the tall porch bannister. The glamorous paint that once adorned the hall is visible only under the long eaves that stretch from corner to corner. Four large windows gaze out from the front of the building and cast streaks of light slicing into the darkness around the hall. At the top of the tall porch double doors grace the middle of the enormous building.

"Listen. That's sounds like Benny Goodman." Music drifts from the hall. Mote taps his fingers on the steering wheel.

"What team does Benny play for?"

"You nitwit, he's a bandleader. Not a ballplayer." The backseat of the Durant shakes as the girls giggle at Billy's inquiry.

Mote circles the hall. Once he finds a spot to park we bound from the Durant. We find our knees tight as knots. Our legs feel like stumps due to the long trip. We hobble through the mass of cars and wagons parked in a haphazard manner.

"Let's see what kind of dancers they got in Jefferson County?" Mote is charging toward the hall with the girls following in his footsteps.

The rest of us bring up the rear. Rounding the corner of the hall we find ourselves passing through more rows of wagons and trucks. Several rough looking boys have settled in around one of the trucks. Three of them lean against the side of the truck. Two more sit on the back. Their attire is an assortment of over-alls or trousers, white shirts and ties. One fellow is wearing knickers. His torso is covered with a fancy plaid shirt. The small troupe passes a soda bottle from hand to hand. The bottle is tipped at each stop. A match flares in the darkness. Making our way past the truck, I watch them mutter and snicker as their eyes roam over Sarah, Hazel, and Marionett. Circling past the shabby truck I catch a whiff of burnt oatmeal and moldy vegetables.

"Spike, what was that smell?" Tut and Billy are on my heels as we climb the towering porch steps.

"Homebrew."

The Gin Town shindig is wall-to-wall people. Couples glide across the dance floor to the soft and slow music. It's like the mushy scenes in the movies. A band is playing on a makeshift stage near the back wall. The band consists of four skinny fellows. They're dressed in dark trousers and white shirts. Most of the band appears to be the same age as Deacon. A peach fuzz faced fellow plays a bass. He isn't much older than me, if that. Four of the musicians are front and center on the stage. A clarinet, a trumpet, a saxophone are snug against their lips. The youngest musician is set to one side of the stage slapping the strings of the large fiddle.

One side of the monstrous hall is lined with tables filled with plates of cookies, cakes, and pies. There is no shortage of folks taking advantage of the sweets. A back door with a posted sign indicates that a privy is out back.

Mote grabs Sarah and disappears into the swaying mass of bodies wedged onto the dance floor. Marionett is quickly swooped up by Runt. In no time the room full of dancers swallows them up. Tut and Billy make a beeline for the refreshments.

I'm set to ask Hazel if she wants to give it try when she is snapped up, and escorted on to the floor, by a slender young man. Hazel's dance partner is wearing a US Navy uniform. The sailor's blue trouser legs are bell-bottom and his shoes almost glisten in the dim setting. I watch as Hazel is soon sharing smiles and chuckling with the young sailor.

"Ain't you a long way from home?" The voice isn't familiar, but the freckled face and the eyeglasses bring to memory our game with Gin Town last summer. The tall, spindly-legged fellow has a head of red hair, like the crown on a Sapsucker.

"Your Tag Silcox, Gin Town's first baseman."

"Never knew boys from Walker County to be this far from home less there's a ball game?"

"Word is that Gin Town puts on a real Hootenanny this time of year."

"Best Alabama has to offer."

Tag proves to be a hospitable sort of gent. We talk baseball and Alabama football for a spell. The Gin Town ballplayer bleeds Crimson and White. When the conversation moves to baseball, Tag seems to know everything about the Yanks and Gehrig, their slugging first baseman. I wish Jack Houk were here tonight. My South Carolina pal and Tag could drool all over each other as they sing the merits of the New York club.

"Looks like some little darlin' has you in her sights."

"Come and dance with me Spike. If I'm gonna risk daddy catching wind of me crossing the county line tonight then I'm gonna dance every song." Maronett is pulling at my arm, dragging me toward the dance floor.

I pull myself away from the Gin Town ball player, but not before I ask a question that has troubled me no end. "How come you catch and throw with the same hand?"

Silcox smiles. "Broke it playing football at the cotton gin picnic two years ago. Took on the biggest meathead in Jefferson County. Broke it just above the elbow."

"No fooling?"

"Yep."

"What happened to the meathead?"

"Rumor is he didn't wake up till the next day."

"No fooling?"

I turn my attention to Marionett. She pulls us deep into the circling crowd. "I best warn ya, I don't dance very good." No sooner are the words out of my mouth than Maronett cringes as I step on her toes.

"It's alright. It just takes practice." Her smile is reassuring.

"I thought you were dancing with Runt?"

"He went for refreshments."

The humiliation and tension that had come over me begins to fade. I'm starting to feel like my feet actually know what they're supposed to be doing. I feel a tap on my shoulder.

"Sorry Pal. I'm cutting in." Runt is eager to get back on the dance floor with Marionett.

Mote is twirling and swinging around the floor with Sarah as the band breaks out "Boogie Woogie." Mote's feet move likes he dancing barefoot on hot coals. He has Sarah Kate soaring around like she's part ballerina and part trapeze artist.

For the next few songs, Mote, Runt, and I take turns dancing with the Walker County girls. After several bouts of jitterbugging I'm relieved when the band breaks into "Moonlight Serenade." Sarah Kate is my partner when I feel a thumping on my shoulder. I turn to find the knicker wearing fellow that we'd passed on the way into the dance.

"I'm cutting in pal. Lane Daggett's gonna show this dame how a real man dances."

Daggett's breath reeks of homebrew. In the dim light of the hall I see that his face bares old signs of an altercation or two. His shirt smells like he's been working in a slaughterhouse. I can feel my hands sweating. My heart is racing and my mouth is as dry as summer road. I smell trouble.

"It's OK Spike." Sarah Kate nudges me aside. She extends her hands toward the Lane character. I watch as Sarah Kate is reeled into the middle of the dance floor. I edge toward the refreshment table.

"Stop. You're squeezing too hard."

I rush back through the twirling dancers looking for Sarah Kate. I find her struggling with the bullying goon. She flinches and struggles against his rough treatment. When Sarah Kate jerks an arm free from her antagonist, he latches on to her shoulder.

"Bet you come over from Walker County? No white trash is turning away Lane Daggett."

"Let her go."

"Well looky here. The hillbilly from Walker County."

One by one, I can hear music die as the band members falter. Couples no longer swirl around the dance floor. All eyes are on Sarah Kate, Daggett, and me. Some of the dancers are apparently no strangers to this bugger as several shout, "Let the girl be Daggett." The bully takes little notice.

"She's just Walker County trash."

"What did you call her?" I feel my chest pounding and my face feels like it's on fire as I clench my fists.

I trip and stumble to the floor from Daggett's shove. "I said she's white trash."

The words are still on my new adversary's lips when I spring off the floor like a coiled snake. I barrel into Daggett like an Alabama lineman as my left fist collides with his jaw and we crash to the floor. I launch a wave of punches with the fury of a summer storm. One punch lands on the ruffian's lip. Blood flows like rain water off a roof.

"Hit'em good Spike. Whoop him good." Tut and Billy are ringside, cheering me on. "Give'em what for."

Seems like Daggett doesn't have many friends in Gin Town. The crowd urges me to "Bust'em good," and shouts of "Atta boy" any time my fist's strike home.

I've scored with several punches when I feel a hand clawing at my shoulder. I'm pulled free of the dazed bully and spun around. Immediately a fist crushes my cheek. Before I can identify the assailant, another body tumbles to the floor.

Mote is rubbing his fist as blood is quickly seeping from his knuckles. Mote steps over the scummy figure that lies withering on the floor. "How we doing little brother?"

"Fine and dandy."

"Looks like we got more trouble heading our way." Pushing through the sea of humanity that has formed around the battle are four more eight balls seeking to knock our blocks off. Leading the pack is a short boy. His pant legs ride well above his ankles. An old dirty Bowler sits squarely on his head. The other three troublemakers wear over-alls. The stumpy ringleader clutches a pick handle in one hand.

"Let's even the odds a bit." Runt slides into the void. His face, masked with a cocksure grin, is eager for a physical confrontation. Runt doesn't wait long for the fists to start flying.

"Didn't your momma tell you that only small children and ladies wear a hat indoors?"

The club-packing roughneck ponders Runt's question for a moment. Only when the crowd roars with laughter does he realizes his manhood has been challenged.

The pick handle is still above the boy's head when Runt disables him with a lightening pair of punches into a pillow soft belly.

The next few seconds are full of pushing, shoving, and haymakers. One of the newcomers is dismissed immediately, deposited on the floor, courtesy of Mote's quick fist. A roundhouse finds my forehead. I retaliate with a punch that crackles and pops. Immediately blood gushes from my assailant's pulverized nose. The last palooka surveys the situation and quickly disappears into the night.

The fracas is over almost as quick as it started. My hands are on my knees as I catch my breath. Runt, Mote, and I take account of our wounds. Meanwhile the whipped and bruised ruffians crawl from the floor. Then, once on their feet they totter to the door seeking a safe haven.

Sensing another attack I wheel around, ready to launch another salvo.

"Whoa. Take it easy pal." Tag is holding up his hands while his face wears a smile. "Lane Daggett and his bunch come looking for trouble every now and then. Sure glad they got their come uppin's tonight. It'll be a spell before we see him and his crowd."

"You ever had a run in with this Daggett?"

"Only once, playing football at a picnic."

"He's the meathead?"

"He didn't get up too quickly then either."

"Mote, Spike, Runt you all right?"

"Nothing to worry about Hazel."

"We need to be getting home." The panic in Hazel's voice sets off an alarming thought.

"What time is it?"

"9:30." Tag is looking at the watch he's pulled from his pocket.

Being New Year's Eve, the girls have an extra hour to enjoy the celebration. They're due back home at eleven o'clock.

"The girls need to get back to the Valley. Pronto."

Quick as a whistle we're flying out of the old hall. The girls have jumped into the Durant as it's fired up. With their hands, pockets, and mouths crammed with cookies and refreshments, Tut and Billy pile in back in with the girls. Immediately the two youngest members of our party begin to rehash, between munching on cookies, the last ten minutes in Gin Town. The treats offer some reprieve from their wailing and jabbering about the round of fist-ta-cuffs.

We hightail it out of Gin Town and race for the Copeland Ferry. Can we find the ferry? Will we make it back to the Valley tonight? If the repercussion for Mote and I will be harsh, I hate to think what storm awaits the girls back in the Valley.

Chapter 17
"The County Line & The Devil"

I feel like Jonah sitting in the stomach of a whale. It's so dark it seems as if the night has swallowed Jefferson County. The Durant sends yellow beams of light knifing into the darkness. Each curve finds me holding my breath as the car's lights peer into the blackness. Glancing into the back seat I see the girls, Tut, and Billy with their eyes squeezed shut.

Runt is sitting between Mote and me. My pal's arms are extended, locked and tense against the dashboard, and his eyes are big as a fist. At each curve he grimaces and braces for the unknown.

I have my left arm hug over the back of the seat with the window rolled down. The cool air soothes the lumps and knots that have sprouted on my face due to the slugfest in Gin Town. My right hand clutches the side of the doorframe and I push hard against the floor with my feet at each curve as if braking the car to a sudden stop. Unflinching, Mote assaults each curve and hill like a barnstorming pilot. Rocks thrown up by the speeding Durant ding and tap against the fenders like buckshot. I hope we live long enough to see tomorrow.

"There's the sign for the ferry." Runt has spotted the Underwood sign hanging in a tilted fashion from a post. We arrive at the ferry after roaring through Pumpkin Center.

"I hope the ferry captain is close bye," whispers Hazel as if praying.

The ferry rest against pilings set in the water. A single light hangs on a post shedding light onto a dilapidated loading ramp. Loud baying and yipping shatters the stillness. No sooner have we rolled to stop than two barking hounds emerge from the shadows. The braying dogs sound the news of our arrival. A light flutters from the windows of a small house set back from the water's edge. Then another light breaks into the darkness as a door opens. A ghostly figure holding a lantern eases from the shadows of the house. The lantern, held high, lights a path toward the ferry crossing.

The light reveals a tall, gawky, white haired man. Behind the man is a woman whose body might pass for a broomstick. The man's face and nose could be mistaken for a teakettle. His slender shoulders and chest are covered with a Y t-shirt. The remainder of the old man's wardrobe consists of trousers and untied shoes. The woman's hair is short as hair on a dog. Her rail-thin frame is covered by a man's over-alls.

"Must be running from the law, or from an angry daddy to be out this late."

"No sir. Just need to get on to Walker County before it gets any later."

"Ya got seventy-five cents?"

The cost of crossing the Mulberry on the Underwood Ferry sets off an alarm. "Mr. Bert, over at the Copeland Ferry, said you'd ferry folks across for fifty cents."

"Well old Bert is a little confused. Fifty cents is the daily fee. Night crossing is seventy five cents."

"We've only got fifty-two cents."
"You got anything worth twenty five cents."

Runt, Mote, and I huddle. We quickly come to a consensus. "No. We don't have anything other than our clothes and shoes."

"How about some homebrew?" Tut's question throws me for a loop. How did Tut come to have a bottle of homebrew?

Tut is holding up a fruit jar. The Underwood ferry skipper quickly snatches the jar from Tut, and with the light of his lantern examines the pecan colored liquid. "Little young for homebrew ain't ya?" The woman's query is more of an accusation than a question. The skipper and woman take hearty sniffs. Sips follow the sniffs. The little sample prompts a sense of urgency for them to barter.

"Tasted better. Tasted worst."

Freed of our last remaining coins, and the bottle of homebrew, we board the ferry with the Durant. Once a heavy chain is latched across the stern of the ferry our traveling party paces between the sedan and the wood railing bordering the side of the vessel. Sarah Kate, Hazel, and Marionette fidget. Our poorly contrived trip to Gin Town has become a nerve-racking ordeal for the girls. I suspect we will encounter little jubilation upon our return home.

The skipper has disappeared into the night when a clattering and coughing erupt from the darkness. An engine sputters to life. Like a long snake a cable breaks the surface of the water. The skipper trots out of the darkness as the barge begins to move. Scampering like a cat the skipper jumps across the widening gap of water as the ferry skitters away from shore. There is no wheel or rudder to guide the vessel. The ferry follows the tugging cable across the Mulberry much like a calf being led by a rope.

"Mister how you gonna get back to your side?" Billy and Tut have been watching the operation with great interest.

"Got my woman sitting by the engine. She'll release the pulley when I signal with the lantern. Once we unload I'll signal her again. She'll put the gear in reverse, engage the pulley, and I'll cruise home. Me and the woman will be snoring before you get on the Cordova road."

The running's of the ferry hasn't distracted me from the issue as how Tut come to have a bottle of homebrew? I pull my young brother aside. "Where did you come to find a bottle of homebrew?"

"While ya'all were dancing Billy and me went to searching that old truck where them ugly fella's were sipping homebrew. Found the jar stuck up under a fender. Snatched it up and hid it under the back seat of the sedan."

The trip across the river is surrounded by darkness. We drift as the moon plays hide and seek between the clouds.

"Lucky for you we had to trade for a ferry ride. No telling what Pap, or Sheriff Cox, would have done had they discovered you with homebrew."

I can see the white of Tut's eyes. They are as wide open as empty tin cans. It appears that neither my little brother, nor my cousin, had contemplated any such hazards. The light arcs and swirls as the lantern swings and a fish splashes as light glimmers on the black water. The towline sags and dips into the Mulberry. The ferry creeps forward and then the flat nose nudges into the bank. We're back in Walker County.

"Please hurry Mote." Hazel begs. She hopes Mote can make the Durant fly.

"I know a shortcut." The Durant hugs the road as we race deeper into Walker County.

Short-cut? I don't know if Mote's really has a short cut? On several occasions Runt asks, "Ain't that Earnest Chapel", or "I thought we'd already passed Dixie Springs?"

In no time one of the girl's is weeping. It's one thing for boys to be traipsing around the county late at night, but for the girls it's a whole new ballgame. I know our female companions will find their daddy's mad enough they could tear up railroad tracks with a rubber hammer. Despite the cool air rushing into the car, I feel my armpits dripping. My stomach is tied in knots.

"Looky there." Glancing through the leaf barren trees we can see the lights at the bottom of the hill.

"*Bump – Thump.*" We've crossed the railroad tracks above the ballpark. The lights beckon us toward the Commissary. The humming sound of the Durant gives way to the whistling wind. The Durant is coasting.

"Why'd you turn off the engine?"

"I think we're out of gas."

"You boys best skedaddle. No sense you having to deal with our Daddy's."

Sarah Kate gets no argument. Her notion of what's in store for us isn't exactly heart warming.

The Durant continues to roll down the hillside road. What had been seconds away now seems like an eternity. Sitting in the sedan is nerve racking. Our ascent into town slows to a crawl. The Durant settles directly in front of the well-lit Commissary porch like a bird home to roost. Four men stand in the glow of the porch light. It's obvious from their looks that the girl's fathers are not there to welcome us home.

I'm on the side of the car next to the porch. Taking stock of the situation it's clear that the safest exit from the sedan is out the door next to Mote. My older brother has the door open and is hightailing it up the road with Runt, Tut, and me hot on his heels. I guess Billy didn't see any sense in joining our hasty retreat. Where could he run? He'd have to go home sometime. Maybe he figures running was only putting off the inevitable.

Roaring voices follow us into the darkness. "Your Daddy is waiting for you boys."
"There is going to be hell to pay. You hear me?"

"Best be on the lookout. You aren't getting off easy."

"Best hope the Sheriff's not sitting at home waiting for you."

My feet are churning up the road as fast as I can pick them up and put them down. The moon has disappeared and the sky is black as tar. I can't see my brothers or pal racing to escape the furious reception at the Commissary. I can hear feet pounding the roadway. I hope it's not of one of the girl's fathers in pursuit. I sense someone heading off in another direction. I figure Runt is heading off toward the ball field. He'll probably double back to Silk Stocking Road and his house.

I'm almost to the end of the road and home. Oh, Oh. I smell Pap's pipe even before I reach the fence that surrounds our house. Pap is waiting on the porch sure as the dickens. I slow to a snail's pace. I can see the vague outline of my brothers as Mote slinks up beside me. I hear Tut gasping for breath as he eases in behind us. I never knew the night could be so quiet. All I hear is my heart pounding as we approach the steps leading up to the porch. The quiet is deafening.

"You boys got a lot of work to do tomorrow. Best get to bed." I flinch at the sound of Pap's voice. I feel Mote cringe beside me.

"Yes sir."

The three of us rush into the house where we peel off our trousers and collapse into bed. We are deathly silent for fear that Pap will hear us talking. No sense in risking his wrath. I don't relish a visit with Pap tonight. Lying still in the darkness I recall the encounter with Pap when we arrived home. His advice about getting to bed and alluding to work strikes me with a dreadful sensation. I fall asleep feeling apprehensive about daylight. What does Pap have in store for us come New Year's day?

"Rise and shine."

I open my eyes. Mote is peeking at me with one eye shut. Tut tries to slither deeper into the bed. The only light is from the light bursting through the doorway. The window reveals little sign of daylight. We tumble from bed. Throwing on a pair of over-alls. Pap alerts Momma to our presence as we trudge into the kitchen.

"Take a gander at Walker County's finest."

Momma is sitting at the end of the table holding Joy. "Good morrrrrrrrrrrrrr." Momma's greeting is cut off in mid sentence. I glance at Mote. For the first time I see the results of our Gin Town skirmish. Mote's face displays two enormous bumps and a bruise. I feel my face. The knot I felt last night feels as big as a buckeye. I discover dried blood from a cut on my ear. My knuckles are caked with blood.

Momma is stunned. "Good Lord. You boys look like something the cat drug in."

Like a strutting peacock, Tut flashes a smile. "You ought to see the other fellows."

"Best have a biscuit. You can't work on an empty stomach." Pap flips us one of Momma's biscuits as he heads out the door. "Follow me." The biscuits disappear like it's our last meal.

We stop at Pap's tool shed where he quickly issues a shovel, hoe, rake, and pick to us. We quickly fall in behind him as he marches up the hill where his watermelon and peanut crop will be planted in the coming weeks. I'm beginning to understand what task Pap has in store for us. No sooner have I realized the consequences for last night actions than Pap confirms my suspicions.

"We need a bigger garden."

Pap's patch for watermelons and peanuts extends along the hillside before it disappears over the ridge top. Looking up the hill I envision the high school football field. Pap's garden is about half that size. Stakes have been pounded into the ground. They mark his vision of a bigger garden. The stakes extend nearly ten paces from the existing patch of tilled ground. The stakes disappear over the ridgeline.

"Working Saturday's, you boys should have the ground ready for planting come spring time."

Once assured that we understand our duties Pap leaves for a shift in the mine. We deploy for our assault on the weeds and brush. Mote and I hack and chop while Tut rakes, hauls, and piles the fresh debris into burn piles. Thankfully it's New Year's day and not a day burdened with the heat of summer. However, despite the cool January day, the intensive labor immediately has my body under siege.

"Ouch." Sweat has found the cuts and scrapes on my knuckles. The stinging sensation attacks my eyes as the sweat strikes me as if salt has been poured into my eyes. Between the cracking sound of brush and the chop of a hoe I hear Mote huffing and gibbering as he attacks the ground.

"They're coming." Tut is scampering along the hillside as he returns from a trip to the burn pile. "Mr. Bagwell, Tuff Ary, Uncle Boyd, Mr. Lockhart, and Runt's daddy. There coming quick."

"They carrying guns or clubs?"

"No, but they got Sheriff Cox. They've captured Runt and Billy too."

I look at Mote. I know he's got the same notion as the one running through my head. Should we make tracks or face the music? Quietly we both contemplate our course of action. Our eyes affirm a mutual understanding. We'll hunker down on the hillside and wait. We don't have long to wait as Sheriff Cox marches ahead of the wedge of our female companion's fathers, Billy, and Runt. It feels like Lee and Grant when the Sheriff and the stern looking elders arrive on the hillside.

"You boys sure caused a ruckus early this morning."

Apparently the Sheriff has command of this situation. "Mommas and daddies were fearing the worst last night. Had no idea what had become of the girls. Hadn't been for the sheriff over in Jefferson County calling about a fight in Gin Town involving boys from Walker County no one would have had any idea what had become of Sarah Kate, Hazel, and Marionett. There was talk of hangings, tar and feathering. Their mommas were in frenzy. These daddies were worked up something fierce."

"We didn't mean no harm."

"We figured we'd get home in plenty of time."

Runt quickly seized an opening, "I told the Sheriff about the ferry crossing. How we had a run in with that Daggett crowd."

"Still don't set right, you taking the girls across the county line to Gin Town. If you hadn't spoke up and looked after the girls, no telling what trouble might have fallen on them girls."

"I'm purely agitated at your boys. The fact you took up for Sarah when she needed looking after is the only reason I'm not having the Sheriff lock you boys up." Tuff Ary, Uncle Boyd, Mr. Lockhart, and Runt's father all nod in agreement.

Mr. Bagwell's mention of jail sets my hair on edge. I see Mote's adam's apple bob up and down.

"Next time the girls want to dance, don't be feeling the need to cross the county line."

"Yes Sir."

Once the girl's fathers had gotten the trip to Gin Town off their chest they turned and trooped off the hillside. Runt's father ushered him off too. Meanwhile, Sheriff Cox lingers for a spell.

"Jefferson County sheriff said folks in Gin Town thought you boys deserve a medal. Seems that Daggett fellow and his heathen bunch been cruising for a licking for some time. Yet, there's a word of caution from Jefferson County. Best you boys don't show your faces around Jefferson County anytime soon. Never know what kind of reception a bunch like Daggett's can arrange."

Mote, Tut, and me go back to the task of making a bigger garden. We are quiet as we labor for the rest of the morning. Only when we finally go for water does Mote break the silence. "Sure glad the Sheriff Cox came along today. Hate to think what the girls daddies would have done had he not been along."

Mote's observation isn't lost on me. The idea leaves me with a huge sigh.

While my brothers and I groaned over the backbreaking task of creating a bigger garden, we couldn't help but feel sympathy for Sarah Kate, Hazel, and Joyce. Their folks were making sure the girls never again wandered off the straight and narrow path. Sarah Kate seldom left the house without her momma, or daddy as escorts. I know she was embarrassed. It was summer before she could leave the house to catch the school bus, shop at the Commissary, or walk to Bible Study without the company of a parent.

"You want to be gallivanting around like a boy, then you'll do a boy's work." Tuff, Hazel's father, had set her to doing all her brothers chores. For weeks Hazel chopped and hauled firewood, drew water from the well, searched the tracks for coal, and skinned any game Tuff or her brothers brought home from hunting.

Don't know exactly what Marionett had to endure as she was bound to her place as soon as her parents got her home. She and Runt didn't see each other for a long time.

Billy disappeared for days on end. I guess things could have been worse than working for Pap. Uncle Boyd had sent Billy off to Earnest Chapel to work Uncle Fletcher's place. No matter how much work Billy did for Uncle Fletch, there was always something else needed doing. Uncle Fletch never saw reason to do something himself when some else would do it for him. I sure didn't envy Billy grueling under the eye of Uncle Fletch.

As promised, enlarging Pap's garden took up a passel of Saturdays. It was the week before Easter when we finished and walked off the hillside. When we were finished Pap's garden stretches clear over the hill. Mote pauses and looked back at the massive new patch of barren earth. "Should've listened to Momma."

"How's that?"

"Dancing is just one more way for the devil to cause a boy trouble."

Chapter 18
"The Cost of Playing Ball"

"Four dollars, and fifty cents a day."
I'll bet the boys over yonder on the ball field can hear Mote
yelling.
"Four dollars, and fifty cents a day. Can you believe it?"

My older brother has just finished his first day working for the
Company. The school is year over. Mote has graduated from
high school, which he constantly reminds me of every chance
he gets. Unlike Pap or Deacon, Mote didn't have to journey
deep into the mine to earn his wages, but has found a job
working on the Company's rail line. He and Runt work for
one of Mr. Earnest's crews, laying and repairing the tracks.
Plus, they also make necessary repairs on the sorry Company
housing and on the tipple station.

"Well Mr. Money Bags, what do you intend on doing with all
that money?"
"Gonna buy me some nice clothes, like a white shirt and tie.
That'll look real fancy when I take Sarah Kate, Hazel, or some
other lucky dish to the movies. Gonna buy me a Bill Dickey
mitt so I can handle Berl's pitches and not get my hand all
busted up."

"That money is already burning a hole in your pocket."
"Like Mr. Roosevelt says, "The more money circulates, the
better the country."

Mote wasted no time in dressing up like a real dandy. I guess
the girls thought he looked real swell too as they've all now
taken to calling him "Fancy." It's "Hello Fancy," "You sure
look swell Fancy." Ya going to the church social Fancy?" I
must admit he looks grand when he gets all gussied up in his
new white shirt and tie.

Uncle Cullie ordered the Bill Dickey catcher's mitt from the hardware store in Jasper. Once it arrived Mote is strutting like a peacock. I'm not sure that the new mitt makes any difference in his catching, but he's hitting the ball like Bill Dickey.

By mid-summer most of the players on the Valley team are making an extra five dollars playing ball for one team, or another, in Walker County. When it came to baseball, there was no problem in helping Dora, Corona, Townley, or Sipsey beat the likes of Florence Tractor, TVA, Possum Trot, or Bankhead.

Tut, Runt, and I have been offered five dollars apiece to play one game for Corona. Mote had been asked to join the team, but was needed on his Company job.
He wasn't disappointed, "Not sure I want my new Bill Dickey ruined by catching that Cox fellow." My brother heard rumors that Cox would be pitching for Corona.

Mule offered the use of his Ford so we can join the Corona team for the day. Runt has been driving his daddy's long red Oldsmobile. Runt swears he's as good a driver as Mote. The memory of our trip to Gin Town flashes in my mind. Heaven forbid.

Fat Poe and Skinny Poe handle the Corona team. The Poe brothers remind me of the Laurel and Hardy characters from the movies. One is as round as a rain barrel. The other Poe is so skinny his body can't make a shadow.

The Corona ball field sits near a coal and lumberyard that has trucks and wagons coming and going non-stop. The railroad depot is directly across the road. Many visiting teams have to endure the sound of a well-timed train whistle when facing a Corona pitcher. The diamond has been cut out of large field that is so immense that an outfielder can run for a week and still catch a foul ball.

Today, the Corona team consists not only the three of us from the Valley, but some of the best players from Sispsey, Empire, and Jasper will also be taking the field against Florence. I renew acquaintance with Johnny Juliann, Buddy Files from the Corona team, and the Cox boy from Empire. I'm surprised to see my cousin Howard. Uncle Lee had moved his family from Dixie Springs to Jasper where he got a job driving a delivery truck for a furniture company. Now, Howard plays ball for the furniture company team. It's the first time Howard and I have played ball together since we left Dixie Springs. This is the best day ever. Playing ball with Howard.

It is going to be a slow day for me, Howard, and the other outfielder. I reckon there won't be many balls hit that make it out of the infield as the Florence team will struggle at the plate with Cox on the mound for Corona.

The game progresses much the way I envisioned. The Florence batters are out of kilter with the flaming pitches of Cox. Meanwhile, the Walker County boys punish each, and every pitcher that Florence sends to the mound. I was jumping up and down as Howard planted a Florence offering so far into the outfield that he could've walked home from second base. The game is winding down with Corona sporting a nine run lead. This is the final chance for the visiting team to escape what has been a walloping of immense proportions.

With each delivery by Cox I raise to my toes. I hope this batter will finally lift a ball to the outfield? Maybe this batter will break the monotony of watching Cox and the infielders monopolize the action? The batter is a kid named Dykes. If anyone hits one to the outfield today, it will be Dykes. The Bankhead player is a beast in a uniform. The line on Dykes is, "He'll hammer the ball, or swing and miss it a mile." An appearance by Dykes at the plate sends every infielder two steps deep into the outfield grass. His reputation for mean line drives has been well earned.

I follow Cox's pitch as it leaps from his hand. *"Whack"* and *"Crack."* The sound of Dyke's bat impacting the ball is immediately followed by a sickening crack. I watch the ball ricochet off of Buddy near his position at third base. Its flight path abruptly altered, the ball shoots across the middle of the infield. Instead of hustling toward first base, Dykes is racing toward third base where Buddy has collapsed in his tracks. Every Bankhead and Corona player is surrounding the prone Buddy when I reach the infield. Tut kneels beside the semi-conscious player.

"He's alive."

"Move aside, hurry, let me see the boy." I immediately recall seeing Dr. Watkins prior to the game. The doctor is either umpiring or watching when Valley boys are playing. The players huddled around Buddy part to let The Company doctor reach the wounded player. I stare at the outstretched body of the agile third baseman. His nose is bleeding, and the space between his eyes appears like a crushed melon.

"We need to get this boy to a hospital. Now."

Dr. Watkins's sense of urgency sets the crowd into frantic motion. In what seems mere seconds a red and black Ford stake truck with headlights as big as stove pots rumbles on to the field with Skinny Poe driving. The sturdy truck brakes to a sliding stop on the edge of the infield. Tut and a dozen helping hands quickly lift Buddy onto the wooden floor of the truck. Once Buddy's aboard, Dr. Watkins bounds onto the truck bed. He clings to the truck's wooden railing with one hand while kneeling beside Buddy. The doctor's free hand presses a player's discarded shirt firmly against the Corona player's fragmented face. The nearest hospital is in Jasper, thirty miles away. The only sound on the ball diamond is the sound of Skinny Poe jamming gears and the roaring sound of the stake truck engine as it races off to Jasper.

"That's the ball game," announces the umpire.

Apparently Fat Poe and the Florence manager decide there's no need in continuing with the game. What with Buddy's life on the line there is not much interest in playing another inning. For the first time in my life I've lost interest in a game.

I watch the Florence team lumber toward the old school bus that had brought them to Corona. The Dykes boy trudges along behind the pack. The Empire slugger shakes his head as if he expects it to rattle, and flailing his arms like he's trying to fly. One of the Empire players places a hand on the shoulder of the distraught Dykes. It's as if telling him "It's not your fault, he'll be fine." I hope the Florence player is right.

Mule's Roadster is buzzing down the road with Runt behind the wheel. The ride home has been so quiet you'd have thought we were in an undertaker's hearse. We're half way to Parrish before the silence is broken.

"Hope Buddy is going to live." I'm not sure if Tut is talking to Runt and me, or talking to himself. No matter. Runt and I reply, "Amen brother."

By the time we arrive at the Commissary the news of Buddy's injury is on everyone's lips. Dr. Watkins had phoned the Commissary so as Uncle Cullie can pass the word along to Runt, Tut, and me. Buddy is alive, but will require surgery. There is more goods news; Buddy's eyes suffered no permanent damage. I feel a heap better as Tut and I trot up the hill to our house.

"Deacon's here." The green Chevrolet is parked in front of the house. My oldest brother and his wife are visiting from Sipsey.

Tut and I approach the house where I can see the glow of Pap's pipe. The sweet aroma of Half & Half tobacco lingers in the breeze. Pap, Mote, and Deacon's voices carry into the night. Their silhouettes frame by the glow of light in the window as they sit on the porch.

"How you doing boys?" Pap rocks as he tilts back and forth in his favorite chair.
"Fine and dandy."

"Come and sit a spell. Tell us about the Corona game."

Tut and I move to the porch. Seeking a spot to sit on the dark porch I stumble over the hunched up figure of Jesse sitting deep in the shadows. My little brother has mastered the art of being inconspicuous. Jesse has positioned himself where he can hear the conversation. Yet, he remains well out of Pap's sight. The last thing he wants is to be sent off to bed when there are great stories being told. I don't acknowledge Jesse's presence as I find a spot on the steps and settle down.

Tut and I recount the Corona game. Everyone listens intently as we detail the horrific shot that Buddy Files endured. The porch is quiet. Only the chirp of a cricket breaks the nighttime silence. Each of us says a silent prayer for Buddy. I keep thinking of Buddy's crushed and bloody face.

"Best you boys get to bed. Take that youngster sitting in the shadows with you."

I'm too tired to heat water for a bath. Rather than feel grimy, Tut and I take turns throwing cold buckets of water on each other. Each splash results in a blast of shivering spasms. Three torturous buckets is the limit of our endurance.

Bed is a welcome relief after the long day. I'm asleep almost before I close my eyes. No sooner have I fallen asleep than Tut rousts me awake.

"You know what Buddy said to me when he was lying on the ground?"

As I shake my head, and before I can hazard a guess, Tut revealed Buddy tearful words;

'I need to play for Windham Springs next week. My folks need the five dollars.'

Chapter 19
Smiling in the Dark

"Spike. I need you to run over to the Commissary and fetch me some white thread. Ask Uncle Cullie to put in on our account." The house is quiet this morning as half the family is working while the other half is cooking up some mischief around the creek bottoms. Tut has disappeared with Pud into the hills with their slingshots and pockets full of ammunition. Mote is with the rail crew setting new ties on the rail line over Patton Hill. Mr. Earnest said he'd make sure that Mote got back from Patton Hill in time to catch Berl in the game today.

Momma's huge quilting frame is set up in the front room. The frame is made of thin pieces of ash that Pap had fashioned from old boards. It's like a huge picture frame without a picture. It fills most of the small room.

Momma collects old shirts, sacks, whatever she can find, to make quilts. She'll spend hours sewing feed sacks for the backing. For the top of the quilts she'll layout a pattern using the remnants of old shirts, rags, whatever's at her disposal. She hooks the backing to her frame, then spreads some cotton for the filling, and finally sews the top and backing together. Sometimes she'll barter a quilt for some goods, but most of the quilts end up on our beds. Nothing feels better than burrowing deep under a stack of Momma's quilts on a cold winter night.

This morning Momma has Joy nestled in one arm while she stretches the quilt backing on the frame. Jesse is her "big helper," holding one side of the backing as Mommas works to square the edges.

"Yes Ma'am." I've finished with my chores, and anxious for the baseball game with Pumpkin Center this afternoon.

Doing an errand for Momma at the Commissary is fine way to spend part of a summer morning. I might see one of the Bagwell girls, Hazel, or some of my pals in the Company store. I'm also eager to see a copy of the "Sporting News," which Uncle Cullie receives each week. Runt's father usually buys a copy, but once he's finished reading it, he'll leave the copy at the soda fountain. By the time the next edition arrives the previous copy is tattered, each page stained with rings of cups and soda glasses. I swear every man and boy in the Valley will have read it. Runt told me that this edition is about "Lou Gehrig Day" with the "Yankees." I hope that some yahoo won't have his or her face stuck in the latest copy.

I bound from the road to the Commissary's big porch ignoring the steps. The familiar smell of coffee beans, sweets, shoe leather, and the forever odor of smoke greet me as I push through the double doors.

"How ya doing Spike."
"Fine Uncle Cullie."
"You boys ready to put a licking on those boys from Pumpkin Center?"
"Yes Sir."

My uncle is getting rounder by the month. His long white apron bulges from his waist as if he's massive chest has settled in around his belt. For the first time I realize that the thick head of hair is disappearing like leaves in October.

"Betcha ya come to read about Lou Gehrig?" Uncle Cullie is wise to my plans.
"Momma sent me for some white thread."

"Well, you're in luck. I've got white thread. You'll find the "Sporting News" setting yonder at the soda fountain. Best sit a spell while I rustle up that thread."

Bless Uncle Cullie's heart. I know that he'll take his time searching for that thread while I delve into the latest baseball stories.

I've finished reading all about the big day in "Yankee Stadium" when Uncle Cullie announces the end to his search. "Here you go Spike. This is what your Momma uses when she's quilting."

"Momma asks if you'd put it on the account?"

"No need. Your family's debts been paid in full. Even got a credit. Take this receipt home to your folks."

"Thanks a heap."

"Hit'um and go get'um."

I pocket the small sheet of yellow paper and hurry home. As I make my way back, my pace slows to a crawl as I wonder at the small piece of paper in my pocket. I pull the Company receipt from my pocket and read that the family debt to the Company in the amount of $17 dollars is marked "Paid in Full". A line has been added; Credit $5.

I'm dumbfounded as I know that Pap purchased his blasting powder and canvas for building ventilation pipes for mine No. 4 on credit. Momma had put sugar on her biscuits this morning. I can't believe that Momma had money to buy sugar. The only way we'd have sugar in the middle of July was if Momma had bought it with credit. Momma only buys essentials on credit. Sugar isn't an essential to Momma's way of thinking. Now, Pap and Momma have a credit with the Company? Pap is a stickler about paying off debt. I've heard Pap say more than once, "I rather starve than be called a deadbeat. Sometimes when my stomach is growling I'm sure that no one will ever accuse Pap of being a deadbeat.

I continue to wrestle with the mystery of how we'd come to be so rich all of sudden. Chip sends Momma some money every month from his Navy pay. Maybe he'd sent enough to pay off the debt. Still, the idea of a credit floors me. In one of his letters home Chip had written of how he was making nearly $63 a month. He usually spent about two dollars a month on what he called "Navy incidental." That included his haircuts, toothbrushes, laundry, and other miscellaneous items. I find it hard to believe that Chip had enough Navy pay to settle Pap's debts and provide a credit as well? Come to think of it, the monthly letter that usually contained money to ease the hardship on the family hasn't arrived this month as Chip is on a Navy destroyer somewhere in the Pacific Ocean bound for the Coast. His letters to Momma are dated several weeks past.

How'd Pap and Momma come to have no debt, and a credit to boot?

I'm eager to get to home as I can't wait to see Momma's reaction when I give her the news. Will she be shocked to see that she and Pap debts have been cleared? How did they come to have a credit too?

Momma is still organizing her latest project on the quilting frame. Joy is crawling around on the floor and jabbering like tree full of squirrels while Jesse is fidgeting like a chicken on the chopping block as he anticipates Momma granting him a pardon from quilting. I hand Momma the thread.

"Uncle Cullie said your and Pap's debt's been paid. There's a five dollar credit too."

"What's that? Ouch." The news from the Commissary has distracted Momma. The sharp sewing needle has found her thumb. Momma's shocked by the news. She never pokes herself with a needle.

I retrieve the yellow slip of paper for Momma."Lord of Mercy." That's all Momma can say as she repeats, "Lord of Mercy," several more times. Each time her cry signals more confusion and dismay. She eventually regains a sense of calm and puts the receipt in her apron pocket before turning to me.

"Take Jesse outside before he burst."

No sooner is Jesse outside than he disappears in the direction of Cane Creek. My little brother is smart enough to know that out of sight is out of mind.

I return to the house to retrieve my ball glove. Back on the porch I take a seat on the steps where I work linseed oil into the rich brown leather. As I massage the glove I contemplate the issue, paid in full. Surly once Pap gets home the mystery will be quickly solved.

Boy, I'm mistaken on my assumption. Pap arrives home from his shift to find Momma waving the yellow receipt in the air. No sooner has Pap taken a gander at the yellow slip of paper than he is out the door with the yellow receipt in hand and his coats tails flying in the wind as he sets course for the Commissary.

I see an opportunity to solve this riddle. Staying far enough behind as not to arouse Pap's attention I hasten along after him. I watch him leap from the road to the Commissary porch with the agility of frisky pup. I slow my pursuit and slink up to the porch, and ease up to one of the large windows overlooking the porch.

Peeping into the Commissary I see Pap in an animated battle with Uncle Cullie. Pap is flapping the well-traveled receipt. Gesturing with his hands, Pap appears to question "How?" to Uncle Cullie. My uncle shakes his head while shrugging his shoulders.

Observing from the porch is like watching one of the silent movies that still appear from time to time at the movie house. I can't hear a word they are saying. Pap's head nods while Uncle Cullie acts like he in the dark as to what Pap is asking. They roll their eyes, scowl, and squint as they squawk over the yellow piece of paper. Eventually, like two barnyard roosters, they turn and strut away as if to say, "This battle ain't worth fighting." Then, Pap makes for the door.

I scamper off the porch and pop around the corner of the building where I hunker down. Once Pap charges past I make a beeline for the ball diamond. I race past third base. Splash. My bare feet land short of the far bank when I hurtle Cane Creek. Streaking past the six room houses I skirt past the Flats while ducking lines of wash hung out to dry. I arrive across the road from the house. Pap is passing the row of six rooms, and his pace hasn't faltered. I dart across the road drifting toward the house and slip around back, taking up a position near the side of the house.

I've no sooner squatted down than I hear Pap gliding through the front door. "That brother of yours says he don't know a thing about how the debt's been paid on our bill. I challenged him as, 'How he can run the biggest store in Walker County and not know who's got debts, and how they been paid?' Cullie says Vera had found an envelope yesterday morning when she went to unlock the door. He said say's that the envelope was full of cash. The cash was pinned to a note. Note said it was for our bills."

"Lawd sakes."

The next few minutes Momma and Pap explore a variety of possibilities as to whom, or how, the account came to be paid. They throw out such notions as Grandpa Gurganus, or Deacon. Momma suggests Uncle Cullie himself may have settled the account. Pap comes to conclusion that Grandpa and Uncle Cullie know Pap won't be accepting charity. Deacon has his own money problems. "Nope. This is ain't their doings."

I slink away from the window. How'd we'd come to be rich is still a mystery.

The puzzle haunts me throughout the day. Only the ballgame with Pumpkin Center offers any relief from the pesky whodunit at the Commissary. I've just finished putting on the white and blue Coal Valley uniform when Mote barrels into the house. He is in a giddy mood. It's as if the Company has granted him amnesty for today's game

A brash and rowdy group, the Pumpkin Center team is clad in white uniforms, trimmed in purple and yellow. The opposing manager is a white haired man with a spindly body. His eyes and nose appear monstrous on his bony face.

One look at Berl warming up with Mote assures me that our pitcher has worked up a real fever for our opponent. Berl's biscuits will be flaming hot today.

The highlight of the game comes in the fourth inning. The Pumpkin Center manager is incised with a call at home plate by Dr. Watkins, who is umpiring today. The umpire listens to the visiting manager's wild tirade for a spell. Deciding that he's heard enough, the Doctor turns away from the rants and begins to sweep the red dirt from the plate. To Dr. Watkins shock the visiting manager flops down on the plate like a man gone berserk, and then lying on his back wags a finger in the doctor's face.

I'm busting a gut in right field when Runt, Jack, Mule, and a Pumpkin Center player who'd been on first base, wander out to join me. We can't stop laughing. In no time, the antics of the raving manager send both ball teams and the crowd into delirious fits of laughter. The appearance of Sheriff Cox finally puts an end to the crazed performance at home plate.

The game's outcome is decided early. Old Reese's "Hurrah for the Valley" cheer is booming by the end of the fifth inning. Berl's pitches are darts as the Pumpkin Center batters flail at the blurs flashing across the plate. Jack, Bud, Mote, and I each greet a variety of pitchers with towering blasts over Black Creek.

Seldom do I hear the crowd, but today I hear Old Reese calling, "Hit one to the bean patch Mr. Spike." The dandy attired black man is smiling something fierce when I round the bases following my blast over the creek. The shot was well beyond the railroad tracks as well.

Our Valley team enjoys the long half innings when we're at bat. Meanwhile, Berl retires our opposition in a three up and three down in seven of the nine-inning contest. The afternoon is receding quickly by the time the game comes to an end. Old Reese makes off like a bandit with his wagering.

Pap is waiting by the backstop when the game ends. "Grab a couple of the Pumpkin Center boys for supper. Your Momma's got a pot of chicken stew cooking on the stove."

Mote and I rustled up two of the visiting players to join us for supper. One was the boy who joined me in right field during the fourth inning. His name is Howard, while Mote had snagged the Pumpkin Center catcher, a sturdy looking boy by the name of Buford.

The four of us set off in a clip for the house where supper is waiting. To look at the table you'd have thought that Momma had set the table as if Chip and Deacon were home. Instead of my two older brothers Momma invited Conky and Pud for supper. They join the two ballplayers from Pumpkin Center in sharing our table. I'm sure glad that I wasn't late for supper today. The chicken stew and biscuits are merely a memory by the time the two large bowls had passed around the table once. Talk of baseball and Alabama football consumes the mealtime conversation.

My share of the chicken stew has vanished, and now I'm looking around the table in hopes of finding a forgotten biscuit.

"We've got a special treat tonight. Graham Crackers and marshmallows." Momma's announcement is met with "Yums" and smacking lips. In no time every face surrounding the long table is licking at the white, gooey, paste sandwiched between the honey sweet crackers. I don't recall having store bought sweets except when I've visited Grandpa, or maybe on a holiday. I wonder, what makes this day so special?

With supper finished our guest prepare to leave. Buford and Howard each offer Pap and Momma a "Thank you for the supper." Grabbing up their spikes and gloves, they dash back to the diamond where they'll load up for the ride back to Pumpkin Center. Conky and Pud soon express their thanks, and head home as well.

The next two hours are devoted to evening chores and enjoying the camaraderie of our pals down at the Commissary. An occasional Clack drifts across the street from the pool hall to where we sit on the big store porch.

We enjoy a good laugh as we recount the frantic episode at today's game. Mote has us hooting when he tells as how while on the job he tried his first cigarette today. Mr. Earnest told him, "You ain't getting paid to smoke." The stories are soon interrupted with the annoying buzz of skitters. They've begun to terrorize our ears. We quickly grow tired of slapping ourselves silly and call it a night.

"Yeow. Ya think the water's hot enough?"

Mote and I have had to draw and heat more water. Tut and Jesse have already been in the tub before wandering off to bed. Tomorrow is Sunday, and Momma expects us all to bathe tonight. It's a ritual we do the night before church or bible study.

"What's the matter? Think you'll melt?"

"Yeow." Mote's yelling and yipping is a knee slapper.

We venture back into the house once we've bathed. I'm worn out from my trips to the Commissary, chores, and baseball. Jesse and Tut lay on top of the bed covers. The room is warm as a teapot. There is no breeze slipping through the screened window. I hear Mote rearranging his pillow in the bed he shares with Tut. I slip into bed carefully avoiding the warm perspiring body of Jesse. Searching to no avail for a cool spot on the bed. I lay on my back staring into the darkness. Once again the mystery of debts and credits springs to mind. I whisper to Mote in the adjoining bed,

"You know that we're rich?"
"How ya figure?"

"All Pap's debts with the Company have been paid. Momma even put sugar on the biscuits this morning."

When Mote doesn't reply I continue to share the events that transpired at the Commissary. "We even got credit for five dollars. You can bet that's how we come to have Graham Crackers and marshmallow for supper." Mote is still quiet.

I'm about to fall asleep when I recall Mote's cheering, "Four dollars and fifty cents a day." Once more I whisper across the gap separating our beds, "You don't know anything about those debts, and how we come to have Graham Cracker's do you?"

My brother doesn't say a word, but I know he's smiling in the dark.

Chapter 20
"Whistles & Weddings"

"Tweet."

"I think whistles have been invented just to torment football players."

"Tweet."

"Yep." That's about the best I can offer Berl.

"Tweet." Another blast from Coach Gibson's whistle sends our football team flopping and bouncing off our stomachs. Back on our feet we race fifty yards across the field. We've been practicing for what seems like an eternity. The first week of practice began shortly after a big storm ravaged the South leaving our field resembling a small swamp. Now, two weeks later the sun has left the field looking like a desert in a cowboy movie. We kick up a small dust storm as we rumble from sideline to sideline.

"Tweet."

I feel the familiar sting of sweat rolling into my eyes. I look at my feet, where due to the heavy feeling in my legs, I expect to see bricks tied to my feet. They are bound in black, high-laced, cleated shoes. I search some twenty odd faces for Tut. This is my brother's first week of football practice. I'm wondering how he's holding up under Coach Gibson's daily demand that, "The Wildcat's will outwork every team in Walker County."
"You boys know those Lynn boys ain't gonna lay down for you this Friday. No sir."

"Tweet."

"Milton if you can't run faster maybe we should ask Miss Crane if she'd want to take your place in the backfield?

"Tweet."

Milton is a cousin, Uncle Rich's boy. Milt doesn't look like a football player. He's a tall, gawky figure. His arms are as long as a shovel handle, and about the same thickness. His running gait is long, and his knees and toes point to the right and left when he's flying at full speed. When he zips down the field his lightening fast feet send dirt and clumps of grass flying up the back of his jersey. Despite his gangly features, Milton is one heck of a football player. Which is odd, because he'd never shown much interest in sports until he showed up for practice one day. Pap describes tackling Milton as like trying to catch a greased pig.

"Tweet."

At times Milton can be a scamp. He bristles when things aren't to his liking. Several times he's crossed the line with Coach Gibson. When that happens, he spends the rest of practice running, and dodging trees on his way to the top of Curry Mine Hill looming above the football field.

"They're fix 'in to settle up with you after that 39 – 0 drubbing."

"*Tweet.*"

"They have been licking their chops all year."
"*Tweet.*"
"Yes sir. They're chomping at the bit to lay into you boys."

"*Tweet.*"

I spot Tut near the end of the line.

"Tweet."

"He's touched in the head for sure. Why's he grinning? Does he enjoy this agony? No wonder Coach inserted him at Center with Gus having graduated."

"Tweet."

"Who's gonna quit come Friday? The boys from Lynn, or the Wildcats?"

"Tweet – Tweet – Tweeeeeep."

Coach Gibson finally ends the grueling ordeal.

"Ya think Coach Gibson is out of breath blowing that whistle?"

I don't know about any other players, but I know I'm too tired to laugh at Runt's attempt to be funny. We huddle around Coach Gibson. We are panting, sweating, and groaning about blisters. Several busted lips are evident in the huddle. The past month has been a test of physical endurance as Coach has urged us to "answer the challenge." Coach has repeated his demand that we not settle for anything less than our best. That our team can be as good as we're willing to make it. Despite the gruff manner, I know Coach is excited about this team.

Old Reese says the Wildcats are a "stable full of thoroughbreds." Henry Barnett, who seldom loses a one on one match-up, is the gutty and durable leader on the line. I think I'm blessed to have Berl, Milton, Lewis Ary, and Red Ferguson back with me for another season. Last season Red earned the reputation of being a "tough customer." Pap says, "Tackling Red must be like tackling a sack of knives."

Coach calls Milton and Lewis the "Pony Express." He exchanges Milton and Lewis like an Express rider switching ponies. Coach keeps their legs fresh. While Lewis isn't much bigger than Runt there isn't a player in the County with his whip like speed. Lewis can turn the end and be gone in the blink of an eye. Today Coach is asking, "What price you willing to pay to be County Champions?"

"Coach we need a few more burrpees." Berl's declaration is met with unanimous cheers."

"Yeah. County Champs."

"Twwwweep."
"Head for the showers boys."

Pap describes Mr. Gibson as "Dumb like a fox." Coach is smiling as we break the huddle. We run with breakneck speed for the gymnasium locker room. If Coach catches any player loafing off the field we'll hear a shrill "Tweep." The dreaded call to return to the field for more burpees.

Showered and back in my over-alls, I collect my schoolbooks and start for home.

"Any of those Long or Hicks boys still playing for Lynn?"

"A heap of Long's, Hick's, and Kelly's been playing at Lynn forever." I'm walking home with Tut. We accompanied by Berl, Runt, Red, and Milt for the three-mile hike back to the Valley. When we aren't talking about girls the conversation is devoted to the upcoming football game with Lynn.

"How big is Hicks?"
"How fast are their halfbacks?"
"Ya think we'll surprise Lynn with Coach's double wing?"

"Here comes Mr. Graber." The rattle and chugging sound of the old school bus can be heard coming past Patton Hill Road. A dust cloud billows behind the yellow bus. Mr. Graber is returning to the high school after his trip to the Valley. He's delivered all students not playing football back home.

We scramble off to the side of the road as the bus approaches. The bus slowly eases to a stop. The thick dust cloud that had been following in the bus's wake rolls over the yellow rattletrap. Standing on the edge of the road we are engulfed by the red dust. The cloud disappears into the steep hollow that borders the road.

Mister Graber opens the bus's large double door. "How's football practice boys? Ya fix 'in to lay some wood to that Lynn bunch?"

"Yes Sir."

"You Powell boys best get a move on. Saw your Momma when I made the stop at the Commissary. She was chatting on the telephone. Must be big news for someone to spend hard earned money on a telephone call? Take it to'em to this Friday."

We watch Mr. Graber motor off toward Oakman. Once again the cloud of dust rears up behind the bus.

"Who you figure is calling Momma?"

I can only shrug my shoulders. I take count of the places I know of having a telephone. There is the schoolhouse, the Commissary, the Company office, the Sheriff's office, Dr. Watkins office, and the Post Office. Grandpa has a telephone in his office in Corona.

"I wonder why someone would be calling Momma?" Tut and I soon leave our four teammates behind as we trot the final mile to the Valley.

"Supper's ready. Get yourselves washed up." Our curiosity will last a little longer as Pap greets our arrival home.

Not until we're seated at the long table, and supper prayers has been said does Momma reveal the reason she was summoned to the Commissary to take a telephone call. "Your brother Chip's married a young lady from Charleston."

I almost fall of the end of the bench with Momma's news. "Why his ship hasn't been in Charleston more than a few weeks." The talk around the table explodes as questions zip around the table.
"Why'd he get married?"

"How'd he meet this girl?"

"Can Chip be married in the Navy?"

"Do we get to meet her?"

The noise resembles a livestock auction at the Walker County fairgrounds. Everyone is jabbering at once.

"Whoa. Take a minute to catch your breath while your Momma tells you what Chip told her on the telephone."

The chaotic state around the table gives way to Momma. "Her name is Margie. Your brother met her at church in Charleston."

The idea that Chip had gone to church without prodding from Momma is surprising. Chip wasn't one to venture off to church unless he was tagging along with her. "One of his shipmates told him, 'You should come to church as there are two pretty girls attending Sunday services.' Chip said, it was 'love at first sight.' He proposed to her on the third date. She said yes."

Now, with the issue of Chip's marriage out of the way, the conversation turns to football.
"Pap you ought 'a see the Double Wing we been getting ready for Lynn. Coach says Lynn will have to cover more men on the line. He says once Lynn is spread out we're going to have more running room against their big players."

"Let me tell you boys, next to Mr. Thomas, Oakman's got the best coach in Alabama."

With a mouth full of Momma's fried rutabagas I nod at Pap's assessment of Coach Gibson. I feel sorry for the coach at Lynn. Even if it was Rockne himself, he can't hold a candle to Coach. There is a sense a confidence in our team. I can hardly wait for the Lynn game.

Chapter 21
"Playing for Grandpa"

"Momma got another phone call today." Mote is huffing when he delivers the news.

I'm whacking at Bitter weed that is spreading through Mr. Bailey's cornfield like wildfire. Tut is hoeing the nasty weeds in the next row. It's Saturday afternoon. Warm soil oozes between my toes as I move cautiously through the field in my bare feet. The first football game of the season is six days off. In my desire to be a ready for the game I avoid the weeds spiny thorns. The last thing I want is sore feet on game day.

Bitter weed has been a plague to Mr. Bailey's farm. Tut and I have spent countless hours this summer battling the nasty plant. Mr. Bailey wants to be rid of the Bitter weed before it creeps into his cow pasture. "Ain't any market for bitter milk." Today it appears the weed has launched another water siphoning attack on the garden. Mote's shouting brings the duel with the weeds to a halt.

Mote's brow glistens with sweat. His heaving torso and gasping effort to catch his breath reveals that he'd run all the way to the Bailey farm. I immediately sense from the grave look on his face that this phone call wasn't as exciting as the news of Chip's marriage. My suspicion is immediately confirmed.

"Grandpa died."

The news hits like a ton of bricks. Momma has marveled on numerous occasions as how Grandpa is never sick. Grandma and Baby Margaret suffered with either cancer or pneumonia before dying. Grandpa hadn't been suffering from any ailments. Before I can rationalize what Mote is saying he continues with the gut wrenching news.

"He just died. He was drinking coffee this morning with some folks at the Cotton Seed. He said, 'It's sure cold today.' Then, he just died."

Tut and I stand and stare at Mote for a long time. The only sound comes from the sky above the cornfield. A crow squawks as it darts away from the dare devil antics of a yellow-eyed Grackle. The black and bronze bird constantly attacks the bigger crow, hounding its every maneuver.

"Pap or Momma send you to fetch us?"

"No. Momma's visiting Uncle Cullie. I figured I'd best come give you the news."

My brothers and I poke the soil with our bare toes. I shudder as a breeze suddenly sends a chill down my sweaty, bare back. I turn my attention back to the Bitter weed and assault them with a vengeance. Immediately the sound of Tut's hoe joins in the attack. Mote has wandered down to the fence that surrounds the cornfield, and returns with the rake that he immediately puts to work pulling the pulverized weeds into a pile. Once our battle with the weed is finished we head home. We've earned twenty-five cents and a promise for some fresh corn when it comes time for picking.

Once church service is over on Sunday Uncle Cullie and Momma head for Oakman to catch the train for Cordova. They're going to plan Grandpa's funeral.

A sullen mood fills our house. School and football practice provide some distraction from the mournful feelings at home.

For three days football practice proves to be the antidote for Tut's somber state of mind. My young brother terrorizes our teammates with his furious tackles and blocks. On more than one occasion an agitated teammate has squared off on a feisty Tut. Coach Gibson interceded before things got out of hand. He doesn't send Tut off to run the hill, or usher him off the field. I guess Coach figures that Tut's soul is ailing.

"If your little brother plays the game with the same fire he's had in practice I can't help be feel sorry for them Winston County boys." Berl's observation of Tut's crazed behavior at practice paints a good picture of how Tut is coping with the loss of Grandpa. He's hurting. So, somebody is going to pay for the pain he's enduring. Pity the visiting team come game time.

It's been four days since we got the news about Grandpa. His funeral is an early morning affair, over twenty miles away, in Cordova. I ride in the back of Mr. Hanby's new Ford pick-up. It's the first truck I've seen with the fenders molded around the headlights. The black pick-up's grill is shaped like a huge football standing on end. Unlike every other automobile in Walker County, Mr. Hanby's Ford has white trimmed tires.

We leave Coal Valley before the sun begins to glare over the hilltop. Despite the early hour, it's hot. The wind blowing around the pick-up is of little relief. I feel my best shirt clinging to the moisture on my back. Mote and Tut accompany me in the pickup bed while Pap rides in the cab with Jesse sitting between him and Mr. Hanby.

Pap has notified Mr. Dutton and Mr. Gibson that he'll have us back to school before noon.

"Wish I didn't have to miss school this morning." I know Tut is thinking out loud. While no one says anything, there is a unanimous look of agreement amongst my brothers.

Hundreds of trees sprout in, and around, the cemetery. Unlike the green meadow where we buried Baby Margaret, the Cordova cemetery is littered with trees that wear the bright red, orange, and yellow colors of autumn. A large white tent stands in the middle of the manicured greens.

"Can ya believe it?" Mote's cry is met with awe as we gaze in disbelief at the number of buggies, wagons, cars, and trucks squeezed on to the shoulder of the road. "Why are the Sheriff and the State Police here too?" Mote's question is met with silence.

Mr. Hanby finally finds a spot to park the Ford. "We're half way to Big Ridge."

"Might just as well have walked all the way here."
"Sure a lot of folks come to pay their respects." Black and white faces fill every open space within the cemetery.

We follow Pap back to the cemetery where we find Momma holding Joy. She stands with Uncle Cullie and Aunt Vera near the freshly dug grave. Momma and Aunt Vera wear black dresses with little black hats perched on their heads. I'd never seen Momma or my Aunt wearing anything like it.

No sooner have we arrived than Pap and Uncle Cullie march off to the large tent and disappear inside the canvas enclosure. Only then do I notice the row after row of wooden chairs set up in the deep shade of the cemetery. There are enough chairs to fill a schoolhouse. Two sawhorses stand guard over the grave.

"Folks if you find a seat, we'll proceed with the service." I'm surprised to see Dr. Watkins in Cordova. He's standing in front of the first row of chairs. A small, wooden, stage lifts him above the gathering.

Momma leads us to the first row of chairs set to the side of the grave. The gaping hole is only a body's length away. The musty smell of freshly dug soil is suddenly apparent as I settle into the wooden folding chair. I stare at the large stone mounted near the large mound of soil. The memory of Baby Margaret's burial bursts in my head. I read the name engraved on the monument. It marks the site of Grandma's resting place.

The rustling and murmurs slowly come to an end as everyone finds a seat. The silence that ensues is like listening to the snow falling on a winter night. I close my eyes. If not for the squeaking sound of a chair I could envision myself alone in the world.

Like crickets chirping, every chair seems to be creaking at once. I open my eyes. Pap, Uncle Cullie, Deacon, and three men I don't recognize, march toward the open grave, straining with Grandpa's coffin.

Uncle Cullie leads the burial party to the gravesite where the coffin is laid on the two sawhorses. Pap and Uncle Cullie take the empty seats set next to Momma and Aunt Vera. Deacon and the three strangers move off into the deep shade.

Dr. Watkins is standing. He's looking out upon those who have come to bury Grandpa. He calls out, "How many of you, or your kin were born with Dr. Guganus's assistance?" I swear half the hands shoot up.

"How many of you, your kin, or your neighbors were cared for by Dr. Gurganus during the epidemics?" It seems like almost every hand is in the air. "We've lost a man who meant so much to so many of us."

I lose track of time. I stare at Grandpa's resting place. I envision him lying in the large box. I'm perplexed at death. How does God take a soul, but leaves the body?

Uncle Cullie is stepping up to the small stage. He shifts his weight, clears his throat, and wipes a handkerchief across his face. For the second time he clears his throat. He begins to talk of Grandpa. He shares as how when he cleaned out Grandpa's old wooden desk he found a cigar box full of IOU's. Some of the debts dated back twenty years. "He never sought the payback promised on the IOU's."

"God Bless," and "Amen" mumbled dozens of voices.

"Is Travis Duncan here?"

"Yes Sir."

The voice originates from the tallest man I've ever seen. He must be close to seven feet tall. His face resembles a young, balding, beardless Abe Lincoln. A pretty lady stands in the midst of a horde of children. They surround Mr. Travis.

"Mr. Travis, you apparently offered Dr. Gurganus a chicken each time he sat with your wife during childbirth?"

"Yes sir. That's right Mr. Cullie."

"Well, Dr. Gurganus cancelled your debt."

"Sir?"

"Yep, he wrote on your IOU that there ain't enough corn in Alabama to feed that many chickens." A hush descends over the crowd. Then a muffled giggle, followed by a few laughs, and then suddenly the whole cemetery is shaken with laughter. That Travis fellow is turning red as fire ants.

Uncle Cullie returns to his seat next to Momma, and Aunt Vera. The somber mood that had preceded Grandpa's last amusing feat settles back over the funeral goers.

"Who's that?" I don't have a clue who the policeman is that follows Uncle Cullie.

"That's Deputy Baker." Momma's reply confuses me. My mind is racing. Who? Why do I know that name? Then like a bolt of lightening I know I've heard Momma mention Deputy Baker. That's the deputy that arrested Grandpa years ago.

My eyes focus on the bright badge. Sunlight sneaking through the autumn leaves glistens on the badge. The man has a thick chest, and his shoulders are as broad as two pick handles. His hair dark hair streaked with strands of gray. His voice commands attention.

"I'm Deputy Baker. Most of you Walker County folks know me, and how I come to know the doctor. I'm here to set the record straight. Dr. Gurganus should be remembered for his charity, and his work to save lives. Not for the speculation, rumors, and accusations that have ravaged his reputation, and his memory"

I repeat the words of the deputy over, and over. The deputy is talking to Momma and all those who know Grandpa. I look past Mote to where Momma sits, and see a tear drop the size of soda bottle cap roll down her cheek.

The remainder of the service went by as if I'm watching and listening to the clouds. It's over. Only with the sound of shovels digging, followed by the sound of dirt rumbling down on Grandpa's coffin do I snap out of the doldrums.

Someone has gathered pieces of chicken, biscuits, and apples for our trip home. Momma and Joy replace Jesse in the cab of the Ford pick-up. My brothers and me are hunched up with our backs resting against the cab or the bedside. The food and silence are the only memories I have of the trip home.

Mr. Hanby drops Tut and me off at the high school in Oakman. Pap's true to his word. Classes are just resuming from the lunchtime break when we walk into Mr. Gibson's office. He accompanies us to our respective classes with a hand on each of our shoulders. It's as if he's guiding us to some safe haven. I spend the remainder of the afternoon staring at blackboards, pages, and words that I don't recall seeing, or reading. It's a lost afternoon.

"Tweeeeeet." Like school, football practice is done in a trance. I go through the well-rehearsed motions of each play just as I'd done for the past month. The long blasts from Coach's whistle signals that the day has finally come to an end.

Come dark, the feel of the bed, and the notion of sleeping is devine. I'm staring into the darkness as I lie in bed. The room is hushed with my brothers lying near by. Only the squeak of a bed, or the fluffing of a pillow, gives proof that I'm not alone tonight. I'm agitated. Sleep doesn't come easy despite the fatigue that overwhelms my body.

"Spike. You awake?"

"Um"

"I'm playing for Grandpa on Friday."

193

I appreciate the fact that I'm not playing for Lynn knowing that Tut is dedicating the game to Grandpa. Once a sleep I dream I'm on the football field with Tut. He is the only player on my team. Deputy Baker is the referee. The deputy tells Tut, "Make your Grandpa proud."

Chapter 22
"The Old Bread & Butter Play"

My stomach has been grumbling since noon. As Coach ordered, I skipped the usual lunch of biscuits, the cool jar of buttermilk, plus the slice of watermelon that Momma had set out for lunches today. A lonely slice of bacon had been the extent of my lunch.

I avoid the drinking fountain mounted on the wall as I walk past the gymnasium. Coach frowns on drinking too much water as he fears it will cause stomach cramps. The hall is packed with schoolmates, and teachers, all headed in the same direction. The crush of bodies in the hall reminds me of a newspaper picture that I'd seen in history class. Thousands of Polish people slogging along a road attempting to escape a German army that was destroying their homes, and families.

"You ready for the big game?" Berl's big arm throttles my neck. His voice booms like cannon fire. Berl is busting at the seams for the game to start.

We pass through the double door heading toward the football field. The bleachers are overflowing with students, town folks, and teachers. It's like wild animals roaring with excitement as they catch the scent of wounded prey. The cheerleaders are decked out in their white skirts and blue tops. The school nickname "Wildcats" is lettered across the front. Clapping and laughing the cheerleaders greet the student body.

"Football players head over to the boys dressing room." Mr. Montgomery and Miss. Crane usher us toward the back door of the dressing room. The room is filled with feisty laughter and red-blooded energy. I sense that our team is ready for Lynn.

We're finally called to appear before the mass of screaming, chanting, and singing classmates. We enter the arena where the cheerleaders have formed a gauntlet. The team prances through the human tunnel heading toward the center of the field. White and blue pom-poms brush my face. I catch sight of Hazel, Sarah Kate, Joyce Hammacker, and Runt's sister Doris standing in the chain of bodies as I skitter past.

I find a seat on one of two-dozen chairs set on the fifty-yard line, and aligned so that the football team faces the bleachers. Coach Gibson sits on the last chair in the front row. Seated in the bleachers are yowling and rollicking Wildcat classmates. The eight members of the school band, dressed in white shirts, or blouses, are playing our school fight song. The rendition sounds like the Notre Dame fight song I've heard broadcast on the radio. The students are in frenzy. I'm soon deaf from the racket. Only the fact that their lips are moving suggests that Runt and Berl are talking.

"Where's Milt?" One lonely chair remains in the midst of the football team. Berl must have taken a survey of faces. I quickly scan the three rows of football players. Milt is missing. I look into the bleachers hoping to spot Milt's snazzy hair and defiant smile. He's not there. Where is our latest secret weapon?

Silence falls over the football field as Pud Jones and Walter Schultz march out from gymnasium. Pud carries the United States flag while Walter holds up the state flag. Immediately the high school band grows quiet. The tap and tat sound of the drum roll announces the flag. Everyone is standing when Walter dips the state flag. Like a large church choir the entire assembly begins to sing as the band plays the "Star Spangled Banner." The sound of three hundred voices singing prompts my body to shiver. I think of Chip in his Navy uniform and stand a little straighter.

When the final note sounds Pud and Walter march back to the gymnasium. The flags snap as they flap and twirl in the breeze. Once the flags retire the cheerleaders, led by Doris, initiate a school cheer. Again three hundred voices bellow as they spell out "W – I – L – D – C- A – T- S." The sound of each letter rings loud against the neighboring hillside.

When the cheer is finished Coach Gibson pops-up from his front row seat. He bounds to a small platform set near the bleachers. He faces the students, his back toward the team. The back of his white shirt is dark from perspiration. The blue tie he wears only on Friday's catches the breeze and swings back over his shoulder. His thinning scalp reflects the glare of sunlight.

"This game is Oakman versus Lynn. It's Walker County versus Winston County. It's Wildcats vs. Bears."

The sound of Coach's pep talk is lost in the cheers and laughter of our classmates. When it comes to pep talks Coach could get the local women's prayer circle ready for a game. The booming sound of stomping feet erupts from the bleachers. The rumbling of the student body cheering drowns out the sound of the pulsating drum and the blaring of the trumpet. Coach's words are lost to the roaring turbulence of cheering voices.

"How much longer till kick-off?" I hear Bert ask.
Only when he turns back to his seat does Coach recognize that one chair remains vacant. The look on his face is a combination of disappointment and dismay. "Where is Milton?"

Runt is next to stand before the ranting crowd. He has been voted team captain by the players. Runt is the smallest boy in the senior class. Yet, his demeanor is that of giant. I catch only bits and pieces of his speech, but I do catch one snippet; "Come November everybody will know the Wildcats came to play." A roar burst over the field. Runt's message has struck home. The team explodes off the chairs, cheering Runt's confidence and trust in our team.

With the rally over we march back into the high school. We still have two classes remaining for the day. So, for the next two hours I watch the dithering hands on the classroom clock seep from minute to minute. I'm required to read each sentence two or three times before I absorb the meaning of the words. I'm running Coach's offense over, and over, in my mind.

"Dismissed." I was never so glad to hear a teacher announce the end of class. The first game of the season has finally arrived.

Once more the hallway is full of students. They scamper past the gymnasium. They burst out of the building. The rambunctious horde sets course for the football bleachers. I exit the hall and enter the passageway to the boy's dressing room. The atmosphere is like a beehive. There is a busy hum as players stretch the dark blue jerseys over bulky shoulder pads. An occasional grunt arises as someone struggles to get a leg through a slim, grey, pant leg. The chatter of cleated shoes parading from benches to the toilets, and back, washes across the room. Occasional eye contact with a teammate offers the only signal that a player is aware of my presence in the room. It's the calm before the storm.

The Wildcats are dressed, and are sitting on the benches that form a large "U" around the room. Blue helmets with three white stripes stand between some of our feet. Other helmets are strung on index fingers where they swing back and forth like the pendulum of a large clock. The team is ready and eager for action.

Coach Gibson summons me to the large blackboard mounted on the wall. He's drawn up a play that I've run in my sleep for the past week. "First play we want to call is the Trap. Give them Bears a taste of Nelson right off the bat."
"Yes Sir."

"Where's that cousin of yours?"

"I haven't seen him since we got off the bus this morning."

"Fine time for him to take a powder."

"Yes Sir."

Coach continues to visit with me about specific plays. His attitude is infectious as the butterflies that clustered around my stomach all day begin to disappear.
"Boys, best get yourselves saddled up. You've got a couple of minutes to finish whatever you need to do before we head to the field."

There is another sudden chatter of cleats as players race to the toilets. I catch sight of Tut as he joins the rush. This is the fourth or fifth time I've seen him heading toward the indoor facilities. I recall Uncle Rich saying, "Ya can tell how good of a hunting dog you have just by how often the dog relieved itself the day of a hunt." I have to chuckle at the thought, if that's the case with football players, Tut is going to be one heck of a player today.

Tut has earned the center position. Plus, he'll man one of the two linebacker positions on defense while Berl will handle the other.

"Whoop." It sounds like to big wooden planks being slammed together. The game has started. Tut's ferocious hit on the kick-off dispels any worries I have about my little brother's ability to play ball with the big boys. The savagery of Tut's tackle has the local fans baying like dogs on a hunt. The Lynn faithful let go with a long groan.

From my deep position behind the defense I watch Tut, teaming with Berl and Henry devastate the first two attempts by the red clad Bears to move the football. For the rest of quarter the Bears and Wildcats hammer away at each other's defenses. Every attempt to sustain some degree of momentum is short lived. Lynn has stacked the middle of the line as they apparently haven't forgotten the damage that Berl administered last season.

Time is dwindling down in the second quarter when Lynn quick kicks after only one try. They intend on pinning us deep against our own goal.

I join Coach on the sideline after he request a time-out. "We're gonna set them up with Four Trap." Spike, on the second play, run old Bread & Butter. If we get free of the goal, run the inside reverse to Red. Remind the boys to make good fakes."

We huddle quickly and then move smartly to the line once I've repeated Coach's call for the trap. Now, I shout out the cadence. Tut's spiral is tight and quick. I receive the center pass and immediately fake the sweep before handing off to Berl. A bruising run by the big running back moves the ball fifteen yards up the field.

My hands feel sticky. Blood?" My fingers and hands are slick with it. I search my hands and arms for a cut or a scratch. Nothing.

"Huddle." Tut has set the spot for the team to huddle.

It's Tut's blood on my hands. For the first time I see blood dripping from his nose. It's flowing around his mouth before finally rolling off his chin. His nose has been flattened. It tilts to the right.

"How you'd come to hurt your nose?" The game has come to standstill. I continue to stare at the mess that once was Tut's nose.

"I think it got broke on the kick-off. It didn't bleed much at first, but then I couldn't breath much. So, I tried to wiggle it back in place. That's when the bleeding started. It'll be alright. Call the play."

"If you say so." The team hurries to the line once I call the play. It's what Coach calls Old Bread and Butter.

The center pass is crisp. I flash the ball at Berl, and then slide the ball against my hip while slapping an empty hand on Red's belt as he flies past. Coach's hunch, and the well developed skullduggery of Berl and Red has the red and blue clad defense chasing the darting pair. With the ball hidden away on my hip I drift around the far end. Once free of the line I set sail down the field. I'm almost to midfield when Lynn's deep halfback sends me flying out of bounds with a bone-jarring hit.

The referee indicates there is but eighteen seconds left before the half is over. We have time for one more play. Like a card shark I'm shuffling the ball in and out of the hands of Berl, Red, and Lewis.

The Lynn defenders aren't to be fooled by another Bread and Butter play. They smother me as I attempt to circle the end. While I'm buried beneath the Bear defense the bantam figure of Red is racing toward the goal with only his shadow in pursuit. The ball securely tucked under his arm.
The half ends. Wildcats 7 - Bears 0.

The touchdown by Lewis is the only score of the game. The second half continues much in the way of the first half. Defenses win the day. Now, walking off the field I search for Tut and his battered nose. He's in the middle of the Lynn team. The Bears are shaking his hand as they admire his disfigured face.

Eventually I pull him away. I have something to tell him. "Grandpa would be proud of you today."

With the game over the Wildcats and the Lynn players join together for a meal in the gymnasium. The building has been converted to a dining hall with rows of tables. Running the width of the arena, the tables sag with plates heaped with collards, rutabagas, fried chicken, corn, boiled eggs, fried okra, thick slices of watermelon, and pies. Coach Gibson leads both teams and their fans in a prayer. He offers thanks and then asks, "that our boys in the military be out of harm's way." Coach's words remind me that Chip is on convoy duty somewhere in the stormy, dangerous, Atlantic.

Mote was able to see the most of the game. He got off work fixing railroad tracks and arrived just as I executed the Bread and Butter play. He sits with Pap, Momma, Jesse, and little Joy. They are surrounded by a handful of cousins, Aunts and Uncles. The gymnasium is like a carnival.

Tut, accompanied by Dr. Watkins, joins the post-game festivities. Stripes of white tape form an X across my brother's nose. Dr. Watkins tells Momma that Tut will have black eyes for the next few days. Tut settles in next to me on the bleachers where I sit with Berl and the rest of our backfield. We're gobbling down the chicken and fried okra.

"How'd it go with Dr.Watkins?"

"Ain't nothing."

"No joshing. How'd the doctor fix it?"

"He stuck some tiny sticks up my nose, and then he started twisting my nose from side to side. Boy, it made a heap of cracking. Just like peanut shells being smashed." I can feel my teammates getting squirmy as Tut delves into his story.

"That's enough. No need to go any further. Let's just enjoy the chicken and pies."

"Amen brother."

While we eat, the conversation is all about football. "What do you think happened to Milt"' It's a question that everyone on the team is anxious to find the answer. Already there are rumors of Milt being kidnapped by other county teams. One rumor has him being hired to play for one of the big schools in Birmingham.

Despite the disappearance of Milt, we have the first win under our belt. Lynn was a tough challenge. There are eight more teams waiting for us.

Chapter 23
FDR & the Barefoot Kicker

"Ugh." Oh, my body aches. Every muscle seems to have been victim of the brutal Lynn defense. I crawl out of bed, and ease into my over-alls. My next stop is the privy. I must have drunk a gallon of sweet tea, plus another gallon of spring water after the game.

I love Saturday morning in the fall. The house is quiet as a schoolhouse on Christmas day. Mote and Tut are probably in the hills squirrel hunting. Momma has Jesse and Joy tied to her apron strings. Once my chores are finished I make quick work of a strip of bacon and a biscuit or two. Now, I'm off to the Commissary.

"Hurrah for the Valley Mr. Spike."

I wave to Old Reese rambling through town on his ancient wagon. The brown horse moves as if he's heading to a glue factory. A cork bounces from the end of a long cane fishing pole that hangs over the side of the rickety wagon.

"Ain't no white team in Walker County can beat them Wildcats. Why I suspect ya'all go undefeated."

"Hope you're right Reese."

This warm autumn morning I find the Commissary porch over-flowing with much of the Valley's male population. These weekly forums exist for only one reason. Everyone has come to talk football and the baseball pennant races. This year there is no pennant race in the National League as the Reds are untouchable. The Indians and Tigers are battling it out in the American League.

The Tides first football game is still a week off. That leaves only Walker County football to be debated and dissected.

"Fine job yesterday." Uncle Cullie must have seen me coming down the road for as soon as I touch the bottom porch step, he is standing before me.

"Thanks Uncle Cullie."

Men and boys are packed like sardines on the huge porch. The Commissary radio can be heard over the droning of several dozen voices. Uncle Cullie has the station tuned to the news where the big story is of a military draft. All young men and boys will need to register for military training. The voices on the porch grow quiet as the newscaster describes how German bombers are leveling London and fires are burning in every city in England. I wonder if Chip's destroyer is anywhere close to England?

"You boys look to be in mid-season shape."

"Winston County boys are licking their wounds today."

The newscast continues. "Fifty naval vessels will be leased to the British Navy."

The greetings and pats on the back continue for several minutes as I weasel through the throng on the porch searching for more "Wildcats."

"Come on. We got a RC Cola waiting for us at the soda fountain." Berl appears out of nowhere. He relates as how Dr. Watkins gave him ten cents this morning. The doctor told him, 'It's Winston County money.'

"Decatur whipped Dora good last night. Decatur might be the best team in Morgan County?"

"We got our work cut out for us come Cordova."

"Look what the cat drug in."

Tut has waltzed up to the soda fountain counter. His eyes already display various shades of black and blue. The white tape that's draped over his nose gives my brother the appearance of a cigar store Indian. He quickly seizes my cola and pulls a big swig before I can snatch it from his paws.

"How ya feeling today?"

"I'll be fine come time for Cordova."

"You'd bring any squirrel's home for Momma."

"Yep. Momma gonna have a pot full of stew come supper time tomorrow."

"You did good little brother." Tut takes another draw on my RC.

"Sheriff Cox found our missing halfback." The news of Milton quickly shifts the conversation back to football and the halfback. Found him sleeping behind the pool hall in Oakman. He'd been there all day. Mr. Cox said Milton didn't smell to good. Looked like he'd been road hard and put away wet."

"Sure wouldn't want to be in Milton's shoes' when Coach lights into him. No Sir."

We turn our attention to sorting out the teams on our football schedule. I mention that Old Reese believes the Wildcats are the best team in Walker County. "If Old Reese say's it's so, who are we to argue?" Tut reminds us on several occasions that Parrish is the last game of the season.

Come Monday the aches and pains resulting from the Lynn game have diminished. Maybe chasing Tut home from the Commissary on Saturday, or climbing in and out of a Company gondola with a tote sack of coal helped eliminate the stiffness? When I board the school bus on Monday I'm feeling fit.

Milton was on the school bus this morning. Despite repeated inquiries as to his disappearance on Friday he offered only an occasional shrug or an incoherent mumble. I saw him again in the hallway before school. Then, he disappeared. There was no sight of him in any of his classes. Rumors spread that he's been camped in the principal's office the entire day.

Nonetheless, he shows up for practice. The fireworks we expect from Coach don't occur. Coach looks at Milton, and then points to the top of Corry Mine Hill hovering over the field. Our wayward halfback never sets foot on the field again that practice, or the next four days. Come Thursday Milton has worn a trail through the pine and oak trees to the top of the hill. It's a sure bet that he'll never get in the game versus Dora as he has yet to practice with the team.

"Gee Whiz." We're playing the first game we've ever played at night. The folks in Dora have put up six towering poles with massive lights mounted on top. The night air and the contrast of the uniforms against the black sky are exhilarating. Everyone looks faster. I've never felt so good before a game as I do tonight.

Dora falls victim to Coach's Wing offense. Coach Gibson knows that Cordova, our next opponent, has spies watching the game. With that in mind we keep our traps and reverses under wraps. Wedges into the line and dashes around the ends serve well enough. The final score is 18 – 0. Coach kept Milton standing on the sideline the entire game.

"We need eleven men on every tackle." Coach preaches tackling all week prior to the Cordova game. He stresses the arsenal of weapons the Blue Devils have in their backfield. "Can't let Cordova run all over us. We need every man on every tackle."

By the time the week is over Milton's dust can be seen rising from the well-worn path to the top of the hill. He must have made over a dozen trips up the hill each day.

The battle with Cordova is of epic proportion. Dressed in their red and blue uniforms, Cordova presents a stout defense as they hold our Wing offense to one touchdown. Cordova's first look at Coach's wingback reverse is in the second quarter. We had dished up wedges and sweeps in the first quarter. It was time for some of Coach's magic. Lewis popped around end and tiptoed 70 yards for the only score of the day. Tut, Berl, Barney, and Red waged a war on the line with the Blue Devils. The four stalwarts manage to keep Cordova's fine trio of running backs bottled up. The only blemish is our failure to convert the point after try.
Following the game Coach expressed his concern for this debacle. This is the second game in a row we failed to add the extra points. Milton, the secret weapon, again watched the entire game from the sidelines.

"Atta boy" greet me and the rest of the Wildcats at every turn come the weekend. The Commissary porch is full of teammates and football fans. The limelight feels good. For the third Saturday in a row I'm sipping a free RC. Sunday morning at church, members of the football team get more greetings than the offering.

Some miners are comparing our defense with the recent shutout by the Crimson Tides gang-tackling unit. Maybe it's my imagination, but I swear I can see Tut, Berl, Runt, and Red's chests swelling up with each passing minute.

———

It's not swelled chests that Coach observes. "Swelled heads" is the expression Coach Gibson greets us with on Monday. Red described coach's demanding practice as, 'He's working us like a chain gang.'

"That was a sorry effort that's all I can say. If you think the boys over at Carbon Hill, Berry, or Parrish are impressed with you all, you're in for a rude awakening." Coach continues to express his dissatisfaction with our 'sorry' display on Friday. Each blast from his notorious whistle ignites a reprimand or challenge.

For the next four days we practice with intensity and an urgency that leaves our tongues wagging at the end of each session. Even Milton's grueling runs to the hilltop seem more enticing than practice. Compared to the practice, the next game has to be a piece of cake.

No mistake about it. The team was not about to endure another week of Coach's displeasure. 32 – 6 is the final score. A late touchdown against our first year players denies our defense the opportunity to continue their string of scoreless quarters. The defense scored first against Phillip Bear Creek when Berl blew through a gap busted wide open by Tut and Barney. He smothered the opposing runner in the end zone. Our conversion attempts still prove futile.

"We gotta lot of work to do before we face Carbon Hill."

"The boys over in Carbon Hill are tough bunch."

"Mr. Roosevelt gonna be in Japer next Saturday."

"Them Bulldogs only given up one touchdown this season."
"Cheatham and Clark, why they've scored more touchdowns that the rest of Walker County combined."

"The President is coming to the Bankhead funeral."

"Them Carbon Hills boys play tough defense."

"They aint' been scored on all but once all season."

"Thursday will be the first time a President been to Walker County excepting Mr. Davis."

"Carbon Hill taking a page from Alabama's defense."

"Hear tell the National Guard and the Boy Scouts will be looking after the President."

I wish the conversation would stick to FDR coming to Walker County. We've been listening for ten minutes about Carbon Hill. It's all Berl, Red, and I can do to enjoy our RC. Once more the cola is courtesy of Dr. Watkins. I take my soda, filled with goobers, and join my backfield mates in search of a quiet spot. We want to relish the taste of last night's victory. All the raving at the Commissary about the Bulldogs has grown wearisome. We settle on the theater porch. The voices across the road now seem like crows chattering in the treetops. I know there is a good deal of wagering on our game with Carbon Hill.

The week leading up to the Carbon Hill game is filled with glowing reports on Carbon Hill's dazzling backfield duo of Cheatham and Clark. The visit by FDR on Thursday has the county buzzing as well. Outside of Alabama and Walker County football, the President's visit is the biggest news to hit the Valley.

Several students will be attending the service for Congressman Bankhead. Frank, Coach's student assistant, will be one of the Boy Scout ushers.

Mr. Earnest is taking Runt's sister to see the President. Some folks asked the Company to buy gas for the school bus. They hoped the best students could go see the President. Uncle Cullie swears the Company would've bought the gas if the President hadn't been a Democrat. Frank is the only member of the football team who will see FDR.

The Bulldogs are undefeated. Like my Wildcats, Carbon Hill's defense is a monumental hurdle if a team expects to beat them. It's obvious that Coach expects to win when we hit the practice field on Monday. We run each of our seven plays at least a dozen times.

Coach throws in a new twist, I'm going to throw a pass off our sweep play. I have Runt and Berl as my targets. For the next three days our offense clicks like a machine.

Coach apparently finds little fault with our effort or the execution of our offense. The shrilling sound of his whistle occurs less often. "Atta-way" fills the air more often than "Dang it", or "Darn" or any of Coach's favorite curses. Thursday's practice is picture perfect. Every play is executed with precision. All Coach says as we huddle is, "Your ready for whatever Carbon Hill throws at you."

"You should've seen all the people, and soldiers in Jasper." The Bankhead funeral had been in Jasper today. During supper Mote tells as how he'd seen the President. My older brother had been working close enough to the County seat that he'd seen the President. Mote thinks Mr. Earnest scheduled the track crew to be in Jasper so they could see President Roosevelt.

"Soldiers were marching every which way. A heap of folks came in fancy cars. Why I'll bet every big wig in Walker County was there. Seen Coach's assistant there too.

He sure got some Army fella purely agitated."

"How'd Frank come to do that?"

"I saw him sitting in this fancy, four door Lincoln convertible. It was a black and glistened like a new penny. Big white tires and canvas top. Mr. Corry's boy Frank, he hops in and took up behind the steering wheel like he was driving for Tallulah herself. This soldier, all fancy with shiny boots, holster, with leather belts and straps, comes storming at Frank. That soldier is so mad; I swear smoke was pouring from his ears.

'Your sitting in the President's car,' he raged. Then he yells, 'That car is off-limits to everyone.' That soldier was stomping around the car, waving some stick in Frank's face. You'd thought he'd stepped on a hornets' nest. I was for sure that he was going to shoot Frank."

"What'd Frank do?"

"He hightailed it out of that Lincoln, and disappeared into the crowd that was packed along the road. I think folks figured Frank was going to be tossed in jail the way that soldier was carrying on."

"I'll hope Frank ain't gonna catch it from the Sheriff. He's a good old boy."

The school day final comes to an end. Finally, it's time for the Carbon Hill game. Coach's devoted assistant is on the field.

The game isn't even close. It's our best game of the year. I connect with Runt on Coach's sweep pass for one score. We convert our first extra point when Tut is given the duty of kicking the point after following our last touchdown.

My little brother is squatting on the field, unlacing one of his cleats. The referee ask, "What are you doing son?" When Tut replied that he was drop kicking barefoot. The official just shook his head and told him, "It's your toes." Tut's kick sailed between the post's making the final score 31 – 14. The Wildcats are still undefeated.

The next two games are against Fayette, and Berry. We blister Fayette 26-14. Despite our showing against Fayette the game is given little attention come Saturday morning. All the talk at the Commissary is the President's signature on a national workweek. The Company, and big business, can only work folks forty hours a week. A man works forty hours or gets paid overtime. Maybe the bad times are coming to an end?

I'm sitting at the soda fountain with Berl and Tut listening to the Alabama game on the radio. The Commissary is busy with miners looking to buy tobacco, boxes of .22 rounds, or smokes. Women, with children clustering around like chicks, sorting through the dry goods or just sharing Valley gossip. The building smells of soap, apples, coffee beans, and fresh bacon.

"Things don't look good for UA," Uncle Cullie declares. He plunks three RC's, another grateful gift from Dr. Watkins, on the white counter top. "Tennessee has scored fourteen points. It's only the first half."

By the time we've nursed our soda pop down to the final sip, the news from Birmingham is getting worse. The Tide is down 27 – 12.

The mood at the Commissary is like being chastised at church. The remainder of Saturday is given to speculation over the Tides chances of going to the Orange, or Cotton Bowl. The idea of returning to the Rose Bowl seems too remote to even mention. The Valley is in mourning when we arrive at church Sunday morning. During the sermon Brother Turner asks the congregation to "Pray for Coach Thomas and his boys." More than a hundred voices respond; "Amen"

"Looks like the Wildcats need to pick up the spirits in The Valley." Mote is looking at Tut and me as we traipse home with Pap and Momma after church.

Chapter 24
Walker County Champions

Maybe lifting everyone's spirit is what Coach has in mind as we finish our hated burpees at the start of practice on Monday.

"Milton line up at quarterback." Coach's order brings the practice to a halt. Milton has just finished scaling to the top of the hill for the second time. The dust from his last journey still lingers over the worn path. Looks of amusement and astonishment flash through the team. The secret weapon is going to be unveiled.

Why is Coach inserting Milton into the quarterback position? Berl had filled that position for the first five games. Milton's talents are best showcased when he has the football in his hands. The quarterback position in Coach's Wing offense serves as a blocker. What kind of scheme is Coach hatching with Berl and Milton? The two Wildcats have little in common when it comes to football. Berl is a runaway locomotive. Milton is like Casper the new cartoon character. He can scare the daylights out of you, then disappear about the time he's set be tackled. Berl and Milton continue to alternate at the blocking position for the remainder of the week.

"We ain't waiting for him. Start her up Mr. Graber." We have a game in Fayette County. The football team is on the bus. We're set to leave for the bumpy, windy trip to Berry. Everyone is aboard the yellow bus except Milton.

Milton's absence comes as a shock. He'd been practicing like a man possessed all week. His dashing moves had teammates flailing as he gave them a shake, or shimmy, before skipping out their grasp. Now he's missing the trip to Fayette.

The bus burps and rattles as Mr. Graber sets the bus in motion. A thick blue cloud belches from the bus. Mr. Graber is still shifting the engine through its gears when a voice shouts from the back of the bus.

"Milton's coming. He's running down the road."

"Let's go Mr. Graber."

It's like Coach never heard the cry. He ain't waiting for anyone, not even a secret weapon.

The trip into Fayette County is quiet. Runt to my amazement is reading. How does he manage to read through the twist and turns along the road to Berry? I feel nauseous just watching him read. Warm air blows through the open window. My thoughts are on Berry, and the empty pit in my stomach. Pray Momma butchers a chicken today.

The swaying and the frequent dips in the road eventually rock several teammates and me to sleep. A sudden jerk shakes me out of my nap. We're in Berry.
"There's Milton. Milton's here already. How'd he get here?"

Sure enough, my cousin is standing in front of the red brick schoolhouse in his stocking feet and wearing his grey uniform pants. His shoulder pads are draped by his white jersey and dangle from one arm. The laces of his black, high top, cleated shoes are knotted and hang high around his neck like a string of jewels. His blue leather Wildcat helmet sits tilted on the back of his head. His thick eyebrows rise up as if dismayed. He's grinning like a poop eating possum.

Coach bounces off the bus, and brushes by Milton as if he's a figment of his imagination.

Milton's grin, and "Hi ya" greets each player as we bound off the school bus while several players return Milton's welcome, and "How'd you get here?" frequently confronts Milton as the players dismount.

"Hitched a ride with Dr. Watkins."

Berry's football team is waiting for us. Despite their poor showing over the past few weeks, they're scrapping like wild dogs today. The first possession of the game Berl and Ferguson batter Berry's defense for ten consecutive plays. Coach throws an early change-up at the Berry defense. He calls my number for the Tailback sweep. I score my first touchdown of the season following the battering ram efforts of my backfield mates.

The game settles into trench warfare. Berry players and our Wildcats threw everything we have at each other. When the fourth quarter begins the attrition on the battlefield is obvious with both teams. Several clean jerseys dot both side of the field. I keep looking for Milton, but he's on the sidelines. His white jersey stands out like a sore thumb.

After Runt has returned a Berry punt to midfield, I step into the huddle to call the next play.

"Coach say's run the Tailback Sweep Pass." Milton is standing next to me. In the huddle his white jersey looks like a cotton boll surrounded by dirt. "He said Runt is the decoy."

I know what Coach is thinking. Runt will be running deep into the Berry defense. Milton will slip out of the backfield while I fake Tailback Sweep. Milton will be my target.

The play unfolds as it had everyday for the past week. Berry's front line defenders are scratching and clawing to get at me. The defensive halfbacks are chasing Runt across the field. When I launch the short pass to Milton he looks lonely running near the sideline.

Milton takes the short pass, flashes down the sideline, leaving the last defender grasping at air, and prances past while Coach stands on the sideline. Coach grabs his ball cap off his head. He slams the blue hat to the ground like it's full of spiders. He almost knees himself in the chin as he jumps like a man who just stepped on hot coals. The next thing I know, he's laughing so hard he doubles up. What in the world has come over Coach?

Tut drop kicks his second points after touchdown. We have a two-touchdown lead.

Frank, the tiptop student assistant, rushes onto the field following Tut's kick. The customary white towel is wrapped around his neck. The big "O" on his blue school sweater declares his allegiance, and his sense of duty. Water sloshes over the rim of the water bucket, the dipper handle sliding back and forth with each swing of the bucket.

"Frank, what was all the hullaballoo with Coach."

The Wildcat water boy, and high school scholar, is laughing so hard he can hardly talk.

"When Milton caught your pass, and ran by Coach, he yelled, 'How am I doing Coach?' Milton was grinning ear to ear when he said it. Your cousin sure can get Coach's goat."

The game continues with both teams exchanging savage punches like heavy weight boxers. Our Wildcat defense rallies to every sweep and throws up a barricade against the wedges, and traps. Every attempt by Berry to get their offense untracked is futile. The game is salted away when Runt picks off a Berry pass. We throw Berl and Red into the line exacting a toll on the Berry players. When the game ends the score is Oakman 14, Berry 0.

Mote had taken in the game. When he spies Frank hustling up the team's three footballs Mote ask, "Frank, if the Wildcats win the County Championship do you think Mr. Roosevelt would let you use his Lincoln for a parade."

Frank doesn't even stop to consider Mote's question. The canny assistant retorts, "Next time I see him, I'll be sure to ask." Coach's assistant is as quick with his wit as my older brother.

"You boys gonna be ready for Parrish?"

I'm sitting on the Commissary porch with Berl, Runt, Tut, and Red. The question is confusing. Curry is the next game on our schedule. In no time it becomes apparent that the Valley is more interested in a game two weeks away than yesterday's win over Berry, or the next game. The Valley can't wait for Parrish.

"You boys are just a few plays better than Curry." Coach's greeting at practice on Monday is a warning. "Best not take Curry lightly." Coach preaches how Curry has improved with each game. "If the Yellow Jackets had averaged five more points they'd been playing for the County championship."

For the next four days Coach is ushering Milton off to the hilltop and singing the praises of Curry. "That Snoddy is one

fine ballplayer. He's one tough slobber knocker."
Snoddy is the pride of Curry. He has, almost single handily, kept Curry in every game.

It's apparent that Coach's warning fell on deaf ears. Curry came out like gangbusters. I have to tackle the rampaging Snoddy fifteen yards behind our line. The blue and yellow clad fullback runs roughshod over our defense on the way to the first score of the game. We should have heeded Coach's words of wisdom.

For the remainder of the first half the contest is a game of inches. Neither team is able to mount any scoring opportunities. When the referee fires his pistol announcing the end of the first half, whoops and gushing cheers blare from the Curry players and fans. My Wildcats are hunched and sullen as we retire to the dressing room.

The locker room is stone quiet. Only the sound of cleats tapping on the concrete breaks the stillness. We watch the door, waiting for Coach to burst in, his face red, while he slaps his blue ball cap against his palm. We know we're in for a well-deserved tongue-lashing.

"Where's Coach?" It's been over five minutes since we left the field. Still, there is no sign of Coach. I look around the room. The team is looking at the door or glancing at each other groping for some clue as to Coach's delayed entry. I feel Berl fidget on the bench next to me. The tap and click of cleats on the dressing room floor begins to sound like hailstones on the roof with each passing second. "Where is Coach?"

"You boys know what needs doing." Coach's head is sticking through the door. Then he disappears like a whiff of smoke.

The room grows silent once more. Players squirm on the benches, then the room begins to breath like an angry dragon. Players stand, slapping each other on the back, or give an assuring head slap to each other's blue helmet.

Then Red is on his feet, and jumps upon the bench, glaring down on our team. The look in his eyes rages like a wildfire. Like knights poised before a king, the team huddles together. "Are we gonna be champs, or chumps?"

"Champs." The roar sounds like caged lions. Tut almost tears the door from the hinges as he is the first Wildcat out the door. In seconds the room is empty. The Yellow Jackets aren't ready for the inferno that consumes their team. For the duration of the second half our offense moves up and down the field behind the furious runs of Red and Berl. When the two powerful running backs aren't exploding into the line, Milton or Lewis take turns causing havoc around the ends. Our defense makes a shambles of Curry's offense.

"*Bang.*" The gun sounds signaling the end of the game. Wildcat's 19, Yellow Jacket's 6 is the final score. The dressing room is full of laughter, bleeding knuckles, noses with the bridges scraped raw, some puffy lips, and a mouse or two. We are undefeated. It's time to settle the score with Parrish.

Dr. Watkins's has left instructions for Uncle Cullie to give any Wildcat that shows up on Saturday an RC. On Sunday, Brother Turner's sermon is how David has taken down Goliath. Brother Turner spoke of how David took up the giant's sword and finished the job. David beheaded the massive warrior. I envision Parrish as the giant in Walker County. The weekend can't end soon enough.

When practice starts on Monday, Milton starts for the rutted trail he has worn to the top of the hill. He is beating his way to the top with his arms pumping. Milton's churning strides are powerful as his torso leans into the hillside. His head bobs up and down as he watches his step, and measures the distance to the top of the hill.

"Milton, get down off that hill." Coach is granting Milton a pardon. Coach's ploy is well timed. The remainder of the week the team operates like a well-oiled machine. There is little mention of Parrish as Coach constantly reminds us of how good our execution is, or how we're in tip-top shape for Parrish.

I feel like the game has been a dream when it ends. The whole week is a vague memory. I watch the visitors warm up. They are a snappy looking outfit in their purple and white uniforms. Some of the players worn the standard leather helmet, others are bareheaded, while others are fitted with shiny helmets. I'd never seen hard helmets until now. The new helmets glitter in the light. Much to my discomfort, I find that the new white helmets also leave a nasty, tingling, sensation when they strike an unprotected rib.

Coach puts our offense into first gear right from the opening whistle. Berl and Red take turns hammering the Parrish defense with brutal runs. Our Wildcat linemen make carnage of the purple and white defense. In eight plays we are knocking on the door of the Parrish goal.

Coach again befuddles their defense when on the ninth play he calls for my favorite, Bread and Butter. We have added a twist to one of my favorite plays. What looked like our tailback keeper turns into a pass when I pull up from my dash, and flip the ball to Runt standing, all alone, in the back of the end zone. Our offense runs as smooth as a fine-tooled locomotive.

In the second half Tut conducts his own reign of terror on the Parrish offense. Time after time he explodes into a ball carrier's purple and white uniform. He demolishes plays before they have a chance to gain steam. He is a wreaking ball.

The field is flooded as soon as the final gun sounds. Wildcat cheerleaders, mothers, fathers, brothers, sisters, teachers, and just about everyone who lives between Oakman and The Valley stampedes onto the turf. Smiling and laughing, strangers and friends surround me. I watch Coach, with both hands on Tut's shoulders, nodding as he talks to my little brother. Coach's face wears a look of homage while trying to sift through Tut's performance. I inch my way to where I can hear overhear their conversation.

"How'd you manage to be in the mix of every play?"

"It's was a cinch Coach. I just watched them come out of the huddle. Then when the play started I went and tackled the guy who was wearing a shiny helmet.

The game, and season, is over. 33 – 0 is the final score. Tut's wait for next year is history. Old Reese proves to be a prophet. We are Walker County Champions.

Chapter 25
"Little Poison & The Honker"

The winter sky bears a resemblance to the threatening, gray, German battleships that have been on the new reels at the theater. Rain has plastered the county for the past week. The hills overflow with water cascading into the steep ravines. Tut and I waddle along the road making our three-mile trek from Oakman. We straddle the small creeks that flow through the wheel tracks and leap over puddles the size of small lakes that stretch across the road.

It's late afternoon as we head home. Mr. Gibson had opened the gymnasium for basketball tryouts. Runt, Berl, and the long legged Hop, are sure bets to make the team. Tut isn't interested in basketball so much as the chance to stay dry and warm a tad bit longer in the school.

The house has come into view. The cardboard boxes that we tacked over the windows several weeks ago are sagging like soda crackers soaked too long in milk.

"Holy Moly." We can hear Mote yelling while we're still several houses away. He's prancing around on the porch and his grimy looking over-alls suggest he'd just arrived home from his job on the Company track crew. He's dancing around the porch like a chicken with its head cut-off.

"Come 'on." I race for home with Tut yelling, "Your splashing mud on me."
We ignore the fence. We hurdle the white pickets and leap to the porch.

"You having a one man shindig?"

"I'm, and you all are going to be an uncle. Momma got word from Deacon today that Juanita is fixin' to have a baby."

"Is Jesse old enough to be an uncle too?"

"You're a nitwit boy." I sneak past Tut and Mote while they're trading insults. I intend to snatch a honey-laden biscuit before those two lay wastes to Momma's pan of biscuits.

Momma is fussing around the kitchen. Her hands look like she is wearing yellow gloves. She has Okra soaking in eggs. Yum. We're having fried Okra for supper.

"Is it true? Deacon and Juanita are having a baby?" Momma didn't need to say a word. The smile on her face is proof enough. I'm going to be an uncle.

I stuff half the biscuit into my mouth. I must look like a nut-packing squirrel. My cheeks are bulging as if they are about to explode when Momma springs more news on me.
"You need to head down to the Commissary. Uncle Cullie say's you got a phone call to make. Best get down to the Commissary lickety split."
"Who's calling me?"
Momma's message has me muddled. Her smile is that, "I've got a Christmas secret" look. "Guess you'll have to go find out for yourself."

I swallow the last bite of biscuit before grabbing another as I head back into the brisk winter air.

"Where you off to?" Tut and Mote catch sight of the half eaten biscuit. They lunge for the door.
"Heading to the Commissary. I got to call someone on the telephone."

Their hasty effort to retrieve a biscuit comes to a sudden halt. "Who you calling? Who you know that has a telephone?"

I ignore the banter. I set off in a trot. Who, and why, is someone calling me?

By the time I reach the Commissary I'm drenched. My pant legs are wet half way to my knees. Water had flowed into the holes of my shoes. The cardboard inserts feel like soggy grits. My socks are soaked. 'I can't wait for spring.'

"I was fixin' to come drag you down here." The husky voice of Berl greets me as I walk into the Company store.

Mule is here too. He's hadn't even been to the bathhouse. He still wears the heavy coat, and soot covered trousers he's worn everyday for the past year in the mine. His face is marred by the usual black streaks. His eyes are pools of white, surrounded by the black mask that covers his face. It must be important that he'd come straight to the Commissary from the mine. He hadn't stopped to bathe or change clothes. His teeth glow like cat eyes in the dark as he grins from ear to ear.

"You and Berl got a telephone call today from Mr. Hank." The look on Berl's face tells me that he's one up on me. I have no idea who this Hank fella is, or why he'd be calling me.

"What does this Hank fellow want with me?"

Berl is gushing as he spills the news. "Mr. Hank is a coach with the Reds."

"The Reds are calling me?" The thought of the Reds hits me like a thunderbolt. A professional baseball team wants to talk to me."
"You and me are suppose to call him today."

Uncle Cullie apparently recognizes that neither Berl, nor I, are in any condition to make a telephone call. He ushers us over to the soda fountain. "You boys set here a spell while I call the operator."

The world has stopped. For the next minute I sit and stare out the large window. I watch puddles explode in small geysers as the rain is, once again, pelting down.

"The Reds. Can ya believe the Reds are calling us? Holy smokes."

While Berl is fantasizing about why the Reds are calling, I also listen to Uncle Cullie make the telephone call. "Yes Ma'am, that right. Thank you kindly."
"Hello Mr. Hank. The boys you wanted to talk to are sitting right here." Then, "Yes sir. Mule Shirley is the manager. He's standing here too." Uncle Cullie is nodding his head. The earpiece is snug against an ear. The candlestick like transmitter is only inches from his mouth. His eyebrows are twitching and bobbing up down like a cork on water. "Yes sir. I'll let you to talk to Mr. Shirley."

I watch my uncle pass the phone to Mule. Our team manager soon begins to smile as he rocks back and forth in his heavy boots. The Commissary floor pops and cracks with every rocking motion. "Yes Sir. They're fine ballplayers. Good Momma and Daddy's. Yes sir."

Berl is no longer hyperventilating as Mule is listening to Mr. Hank. There are long pauses as Mule listens and ponders over the conversation. "No sir. The Houk boy lives in South Carolina. He plays in the Valley when he's visiting his granddad and grandma in the summer. Yes Sir. Nelson is a hard throwing boy. His straight pitch got a tail that stretches halfway across the diamond.

The conversation goes on. "Yes Sir." Best eye I ever seen on a schoolboy. Blasted one that would've been out of Rickwood. Seen a month or two go by where no pitcher can strike him out. Mr. Hank, he's the closest I've ever seen to the oldest Walker boy."

The longer Mule talks the faster his rocking accelerates. The old wooden floor is squeaking and popping something fierce.

"Yes sir."

"Spike, Mr. Hank wants to talk to you."

My hands are sweaty. They're nearly as bad as the time I walked Sarah Kate home from the bus stop. I take the telephone. The telephone snaps, and crackles, while Mr. Hanks tells of how the Red's had come by my name. How Mr. Walker had watched me play against Sipsey and Bankhead. We chat for a spell about the Reds minor league teams. We talk about school. I explain that I'll be finished with my requirements next month. Then he asks me the best question I've ever been asked.

"How'd you like to come to Birmingham this summer and workout for the Barons?

"Yes sir. I'd like that a lot. Yes sir. Thank you."
I hand the skinny black phone to Berl. My tough pal's hands are shaking as he fumbles with the two pieces of the telephone.

"Yes sir."

Berl carries on a conversation with Mr. Hank. His posture stiffens, and his eyes sparkle. The conversation between Berl and Mr. Hank seems to be running in the same direction mine had gone.

"Yes sir. Much appreciated."

Berl hands the phone back to Uncle Cullie. My uncle advises Mr. Hank as to where to send any mail. Bert is slapping me on the back until I'm almost out of breath.

"We'll be playing with Little Poison and The Honker." There is no mistaking Berl's excitement.

"This calls for a celebration."

The RC Cola is courtesy of Uncle Cullie, and it's the best ever.

"Thanks a heap Uncle Cullie."

When the soda is gone Berl and I beat it for home. We slosh through the deep puddles. The drenching rain fails to dampen our spirits. We can't wait to tell our folks the news. We can't wait for the day when we'll go to Rickwood. It's a dream come true.

Chapter 26
"One Day Too Many"

"Charleston? Why are you heading to Charleston?"

"Got a job guarding the shipyard."

Deacon and Juanita have shown up for our ball game with
TVA. My sister-in-law's belly is showing a small bump. The
news that Deacon and Juanita will be leaving for South
Carolina has everyone feeling chipper. There is also the glum
realization that the war in Europe is splitting the family once
more. It's saddening to hear that my oldest brother and his
family will be leaving Walker County. Still we're excited that
Deacon has escaped the grueling struggles and hazards of coal
mining.

Deacon has to be in Charleston in ten days. He and Juanita
have decided that she will stay in Sipsey until the baby
arrives. She will have her sisters, and Dr. Watkins, to look
after her. Momma is pleased as punch when she learns that
the first grandchild will be close at hand when it's born.

The news of my brother's job is just the latest sign that the
threat of war looms over the horizon. Some of my pals and
teammates have already left school and the Valley. Factories,
mills, and mines are scrambling to fill the growing number of
new jobs. The familiar faces of the Cicero's, Jake Millwood,
Runt, and Conky no longer dot our ball team. Outside of Jack,
Berl, and myself, the Valley team is made up of younger
players like Tut, and Pud. Plus, hired players from Townley,
Sipsey, Parrish, or one of the other county teams.

The Valley isn't the only team hurting for players. Berl and I
have been recruited on more than one occasion to play for
teams such as Prospect, Eldridge, and Oakman.

The game today is a novelty for me. I watch Berl warm up. Cecil Brannon is catching, and is the oldest player on the field today. The aging catcher went to school with Deacon.

This is the first day in over a week that the gaunt looking miner won't be pulling coal out of the mine. This is also the first Valley game that I've ever played that Mote isn't catching. I miss the sound of his laughter and incessant chatter behind the plate. The comfortable assurance I've derived from my teammates the past four summers is missing.

TVA throws two pitchers at us. One, who they call "Wig," is rumored to have been playing in the Alabama State League before joining the TVA team. Lefty is the other pitcher. He's a curly haired ballplayer that's taller than a courthouse statue, and has hands as big as ham hocks. An enormous hand conceals the ball so that it can't be seen until Lefty lets fly.

The TVA pitchers are a nightmare for The Valley. When the game ends they have struck out sixteen Valley batters. The TVA pitchers fail to strike me out, but I manage only one hit. My hit is greeted by a "Hurrah for the Valley." That hit accounts for our only runs of the day. The final score is 5 – 2. Berl has only given up five hits. The bad news is our patchwork team makes more errors than a first year student in Mrs. Corry's typing class.

The game over, I'm sitting in the outfield grass eating egg sandwiches and drinking sweet tea with our family. While we eat, Deacon shares the fantastic details of his new job. He'll work forty hours a week, with overtime. He'll be checking credentials for possible saboteurs. He'll also be issued a pistol to discourage sabotage as well as deterring folks from stealing government goods. He and Juanita will have a home with running water. Plus, an electric stove. Juanita is plum ecstatic about having indoor plumbing like the houses on Silk Stocking Road.

"Sure sounds like a long way from The Valley what with indoor plumbing and spies."

Pap recounts the latest news from Chip. His last letter described his trip to England. His letter praises the determination of the British. They are standing firm despite the brutal bombings that continue to demolish their cities. Chip also sends news that Margie has joined the military too. She is now a member of the Coast Guard.

While Pap is catching up on Chip, Uncle Cullie has strolled over to our family social.

"Got a letter for you Spike. Come all the way from Ohio."

"Who do I know in Ohio?" The thought no sooner enters my mind than I realize that Cincinnati is in Ohio. It's from the Reds.

My arms tingle as if I'd just pounded a pitch over Black Creek. The family circle is hushed as I take the letter from Uncle Cullie. My name is printed on the envelope. In the bold letters in the corner of the envelope I read, Cincinnati Reds. I'm holding my breath as I fumble with the envelope. I contemplate what the contents might reveal.

"If you open the envelope it will be easier to read the letter." Pap is extending his black handled pocketknife to me.

Like dressing a rabbit for Momma, I carefully pierce the flap and ease the blade along the crease. With the envelope open I retrieve the single sheet of folded paper. I almost laugh when I see Cincinnati in big red letters printed on the thick stationary.

"Ya gonna keep it a secret, or do we get to know what the

Reds have to say?"

"Rickwood in August. The Reds want me at Rickwood for a tryout in August."

The idea of playing ball in Rickwood lifts me off my feet. My voice seems incapable of sound. I pass the letter to Pap. "Sure enough. It's an invite from Cincinnati. Congratulations boy."

"Thanks Pap."

Pap's face is gleaming. I feel a knot in my throat as I recall Mr. Ozzie telling how Pap had forgone a chance to play professional baseball. Pap realizes that I have the opportunity he had to pass on so long ago. I can hardly wait for August. I have two months to dwell on the baseball tryout. Berl and Jack will be going along with me. The three of us will be making the trip to Rickwood. Apparently Cincinnati thinks they have found some potential ballplayers in The Valley. August sure seems like a long way away.

The weeks seem to drag by as every soul in the Coal Valley is staggered by the smothering heat beating down on the county. The only relief from the boiler like heat comes when black, billowing, clouds swoop over the hills. The mushrooming clouds are laced with lightning and thunderstorms that shake every house to the foundation.

Today, a new storm has driven me away from hoeing on the Bailey farm. I'm losing the race to beat the storm home. With the raindrops growing to the size of buckeyes I concede the race to the gully washer. I seek safety and comfort at the Commissary. The long porch is littered with folks seeking cover from the deluge. Now long, frightening bolts are crashing around Coal Valley.

"How you doing Spike?" Mr. Earnest is leaning against one of the large posts, staring at the sheets of water blowing across the road. Runt's father wears his usual fedora, white shirt, and brown suit. His suit is garnished with the customary black tie of a Company administrator.

"Good as can be. Mr. Earnest."

"You been working?"
"Yes sir. Working for Mr. Bailey."

"Hummm. Would you be interested in mining for the Company?"

Mr. Earnest's proposal strikes me with a whirlwind of emotions. On one account, I'm apprehensive about being in stuck in a black hole. Yet, miners are making six dollars a day. I quickly do the figuring. I can make over thirty dollars a week. Maybe more if the Union and the Company agree on the one-dollar wage increase that's been rumored? No question that Momma and Pap can use the extra money.

"You think on it a spell. Let me know in the next day, or two."

"Yes sir. Thanks a heap."

Mr. Earnest and I talk about the TVA game. Then, he tells how the war in Europe is making it harder for the Company to find men to work the mines. The mills and factories are paying better wages up north. Some of the miners have packed up their families and headed for places like Birmingham, Chicago, and Detroit. The factories and mills can't hire enough people. Even the black miners are packing up. Like everyone else, they are heading north with the promise of higher wages.

"If that keeps up we'll have to hire prisoners from the state to work the mines. I hope we don't stoop to that notion again."

The storm is letting up, and as the Commissary porch is abandoned I bid Mr. Earnest, "Thanks for the offer," and then I make for home with my feet sloshing in the flooded road.

The apprehensive idea of coal mining gnaws at me. I reflect on the stories and experiences I've heard Uncle Rich, Deacon, and Pap tell. I try to envision the daily grind of mining. Where will this road take me?

"Lord a Mercy." The alarmed tone of Momma's voice is accompanied by the sound of a spoon crashing into a bowl. No sooner have I shared the news of Mr. Earnest job offer than Momma is fit to be tied. "The Good Lord just answered my prayers. My oldest boy is finally free of that miserable job. Now, you tell me that I got another fool that wants to sell his soul to the Company? Heaven forbid."

The rest of supper is consumed in silence. Tut and I are feeding chickens and collecting water for Momma when the smell of the Half and Half pipe tobacco alerts me to Pap's presence on the back porch.

"You're old enough to decide for yourself. You can't please everyone. In this case your Momma. Mothers fret about their children growing up. It's just a matter of fact. It's hard for them to let go. Comes a time when you have to do what you think is best for you. If mining is something you feel the need to consider, then so be it."

The morning air is fresh with the scent of Loblolly. The rain has left the Valley smelling like a clean shirt. I catch Mr. Earnest heading to the Company office. We agree that I'll start tomorrow. He say's as how Pap works a morning shift, that he'll put me on an afternoon shift. "No sense in having your Momma worrying about two of her men being in the mine at the same time."

I lay in bed tossing and turning for what seems most of the night. I feel antsy as if I'm lining up for a Parrish kick-off. I'll be working an afternoon shift in Mine No. 4 tomorrow.

The squeaking floorboards shake me from my light slumber. It's Pap moving around the house. He's working the morning shift. The sound of a chair sliding across the kitchen floor tells me that Pap has tied his shoes, and then his footsteps approach the doorway. He opens the door.

"It's a new day." I yank the covers from my brother, and roll off the bed.

I rake the rain caked front yard before I join the family at the table. Momma has an egg for each of us, plus the usual pan of biscuits. When Pap swipes a chunk of biscuit into the last of the eggs yellow drippings I seize the chance to ask the questions that had kept me awake all night.

"Pap. How do you know who's is who in the mine? How do you know it's not Uncle Rich, or one of the Cicero's?

"I reckon I've just come to recognize how a fella walks. Sometimes, I see how he goes about his job. Knowing what job a man is doing, or where he's working in the mine can tell me who's there. The sound of a voice can tell me which miner I've come across."

I swallow the final bite of biscuit. It feels like it's stuck in my throat.

Come afternoon I take up the old lunch bucket that Momma has filled with biscuits, strips of bacon, and a bottle of water. Momma hadn't said where she'd come across the pail. I hope it didn't belong to a miner who'd been killed or hurt badly in an accident? On the back porch I find the quilted hat, waist length coat, thick trousers, and heavy boots that Deacon no longer needs. The coat and trousers have been scrubbed and flushed with creek water. They still feel like tree bark. I set off for my first day as a coal miner with the coat and trousers bundled under one arm. The boots are laced together. I throw them over my shoulder. My first destination is the Company bathhouse.

The bathhouse sits above Tut's favorite fishing hole. The bathhouse is where I'll join the shift of miners exchanging their over-alls for the rugged, soot covered, pants and coats they will wear into Mine No. 4. The bathhouse is like a barn. From the rafters chains hang like vines flowing down from a tree. Each chain can be lowered and raised on a small pulley, and on each chain is a hook with a numbered metal tag. I've been given tag number 11. I don't ask whom number 11 belonged to before Mr. Earnest handed it to me.

What a relief to find that Uncle Rich and Gus Cicero will be working this shift with me. Their presences eases my feelings of isolation and the sense of doom I've had for the past two days.

I strip down to my "birthday suit" as Uncle Rich describes a naked body. I pull on the old Long Johns, and Deacon's well-worn coat, trousers, and boots. With the hat mounted on my head I slip a carbide light over the bill and around the cap's crown. I'd found the used carbide light at the Commissary, and paid Uncle Culley twenty-five cents for it. Every miner wears a carbide light, which pokes holes in the black caverns. The dim, yellow, glow guides the way into and out of the mine.

I clip the metal tag to my over-all then I crank the bundle of my clothes into the rafters and join Uncle Rich, Gus, and the small army of miners marching toward Mine No. 4. Despite the warm afternoon sun and the heavy clothes I shiver. The sweat on my back is chilling. A nauseating feeling grips my stomach as we scale the small mountain.

At the mouth of the mine we mount the man trip. The small, flat, trolley is mounted on rails that lead into Mine No. 4. Spying the entrance I feel like the Pharaoh's army at the Red Sea. I watch the daylight dwindle as we journey deeper into the darkness.

"Your light."

"Huh?"

"Turn on your light."
When we had climbed aboard the small flat trolley I neglected to turn on my carbide light. In the dimming light the miner's carbide lights glow like lightening bugs. The trolley shakes and rumbles deeper into the man made cavern. I glance back. The light filtering through the entrance grows smaller and smaller. Finally the mine's mouth appears like a cat's eye glowing in the dark. Then the daylight is gone.

With a sudden jerk the trolley comes to stop with an ear-piercing screech. I slip off the man trip with the rest of the miners. Plodding and stumbling, I follow the bobbing light of Uncle Rich. The beam from my light bounces and jiggles between the broken floor and the back of Uncle Rich's coat. Like a drunk on Saturday night I stumble along.
"Don't hurt yourself boy." The sound of Gus's hee-haw laughter brings more amused cackles from the darkness.

The cavern extends deeper into the side of the mountain. We walk into another branch of the mine. Here I'll begin coal mining. My shift is just beginning and already the sweat is dripping down my face despite the dampness that lingers in the chamber.
"Here's where you start." I come to a stop with Gus's hand on my shoulder. I turn my head from side to side. Only black walls and a wooden barricade fill the feeble light beam.

The pile of broken coal tells me that this is where Berl's father had set a charge. The shooter has turned a stone wall into a pile of boulders. Here my shift will break, heft, and load trolleys for the trip to the tipple station.

I set about my new job as a loader. Despite the grueling work I feel like an animal trapped in a box. The roof seems to be bearing down on me. The water seeping from the cracks and crevices appears to flow with more frequency. Each bang of the coal trolleys colliding provides a momentary sense of panic as I imagine a gas explosion. With every unusual smell or brackish taste detected in my mouth, I suspect methane. Where is that canary?

After what feels like several days Uncle Rich appears out of the blackness. "Best take time for your dinner if you're going to make it through the second half of your shift."
Uncle Rich is telling me that we've only finished half the shift?

239

Good Lord.

I wander back to where I think I've placed my lunch pail. I'm almost frantic when I finally locate the small bucket. With the same eagerness that I'd have for Momma's Sunday supper, I delve into the biscuit.

"Huh?"

The glow of the carbide light reveals a black ring around my biscuit. I quickly study the mysterious line that circles the biscuit. I start fuming at what has been a grievous form of monkeyshines. Some miner has fouled my lunch.

I'm fixing to find the culprit when Uncle Rich appears out of the darkness once more. "What got your goat? Your nostrils are flaring like a ornery mule."

"Look at what some nitwit did to my biscuits."

Uncle Rich takes my biscuit. He turns it over in his hands, and surveys the biscuit like he expected to find gold. Finally a small grin breaks out beneath the black dust that covers his face. "Spike. Take another bite of this biscuit."

I take the biscuit, and take a huge bite. "Look at your biscuit."

A second line now intersects what remains of the first line. What? Then the realization strikes home. There have been no monkeyshines. My lips had formed the black ring around the biscuit. Pap had always said that miners breathe, and eat coal dust.

Uncle Rich slaps my shoulder as he sets out to find his own lunch bucket. I can see his light bobbing in the darkness when he turns back. His light beam probes the darkness until it settled back on me. "Your Pap is going to get a kick out of this story."

For the remainder of the day I labor at my job. All the while I shiver in the dark, dank, cavity. How do Pap, Uncle Rich, and the Cicero's deal with this confinement every day? Do they ever get use to the chill, the threat of falling rocks, gas, or a cave-in?

The hum of the electric motor that powers the man trip is music to my ears. My shift is over. I jump aboard as if I escaping the devil himself. I squint as the man trip rolls into the daylight. Halleluah.

Standing beneath the warm water cascading from the pipes feeding the bathhouse I watch a stream of black water roll down my legs, around my feet, and between my toes before flooding into the gaps that dot the bathhouse floor. I feel almost normal as I towel off.

I watch the other members of my shift as the black coal dust is washed away. When moments before the faces had been coated with black dust, they now suddenly appear white and pasty as if freed from a coffin. The mood in the bathhouse is light. One more grueling day is over. Each miner has six more dollars in which to pay off his Company debt. Hopefully there will be enough left over to put a few more meals on the table.

The chain that holds my clothes clatters as I pull it down. The small pulley wheezes like a man struggling for breath. I throw on the faded blue shirt, and jump into my over-alls. I bundle up the hand-me-down coat and trousers, and lace the heavy boots together before draping them over my shoulder. I hang the carbide light on a nail protruding from the bathhouse wall.

241

I step outside. Summer heat radiates from the ground. A warm current eases through my body. The earth flakes beneath my bare feet. The warmth soothes the blisters and welts on my feet raised by the heavy boots.

"Spike. You forgot your carbide."
I don't look back to see who discovered the light hanging on the nail. I offer a dismissing wave.

"No. I didn't forget it. I won't be needing it again."

I stop at the Company office. Mr. Earnest is there. "Mr. Earnest. I don't want mean to leave you short handed, but I don't plan on working another day in the mine."

"Spike. I seen men who've worked the mines for half their life walk out one day, and swear they're never gonna set foot in a mine again. A mine can drive a man crazy. Best you found out now while you still got your youth."

I give Momma the six dollars that Mr. Earnest paid me for the day. I tell Pap that I'd resigned my job as a coal miner.

"Don't fret. Seen men shaking so bad they couldn't get off the man trip. Uncle Rich said you did a day's work for a day's pay. That's all anyone can ask."

The day is over. Lying in bed, I stare at the splash of moonlight sneaking through the cracks in the wall. I imagine the clatter of the man trip. I shiver as I recall the darkness closing in on me, and chilling sweat running down my back.

I hope that Mr. Bailey still needs help with hoeing and cotton picking. One day in the mine was one day too many.

Chapter 27
"It's Not a Dream"

I grab an inch of skin on my forearm and pinch myself. No. I'm not dreaming. The large white letters above the arched entry read Rickwood Field. I'm not sure that Momma would approve if I told her Rickwood's gates looked like the gates of heaven. The entrance into the stadium resembles a big city church, or movie theater.

The sky was still dark when we left The Valley. Mule has driven us to Rickwood in his Roadster. Mr. Earnest had Mule gas up his Ford at the Company shops in order for us to make the trip. We're jammed into the Roadster as two additional Walker County boys are making the trip. Charlie McClinton and Gus Cicero. They're both looking to get out of the mines. Playing ball offers the best escape.

Charlie has played for the Valley, and just about every team in Walker County. He has a penchant for turning singles into doubles, and he can throw a ball like it's been fired from a cannon. He and I had played together against Florence two weeks past. I watched him field a ball on the bank of Black Creek. Florence had a runner tagging up at third base. Charlie threw the runner out by ten feet. Like Berl, Charlie makes more money playing ball on weekends than a coal miner makes in two days.

Gus has been a teammate for most of my life. He's the steady influence on the team when things aren't going so good. He can play any position with skill and savvy, and can swing a bat with the best of them.

"Holy smoke."
"Ain't it something?"

My teammates are gawking at the stadium as if they've discovered a grand monument in the desert.

"Let me remind you boys that Rickwood ain't no different that the ball field back home. You've been playing on ball diamonds all summer. It's got a home plate, three bases, a pitching mound, and ninety feet between the bases. It's a ball field. Just play ball. Forget about the fancy seats, benches, and such. Just go do what you been doing since the day you discover how to breathe." I nod at Mule's advice. The other four hopefuls acknowledge Mule's pearls of wisdom.

The brick layered street next to the stadium is lined with a variety of trucks and sedans. A couple of wagons rest alongside the road; the mules are tethered to a post. Mounted on the post is a "Burma Shave" sign. Mule finds a spot near the stadium where he can park the Roadster in the shade of massive pin oak. We're wearing our white Valley uniforms as Mr. Earnest suggested. My teammates each wear a Valley cap. The faded and stretched Baron's cap that Grandpa had given to me years ago sets atop my head.

Taking up our gloves, spikes, and bats we follow Mule through the stadium entry. The passageway is dark, and slopes gently into the bowels of the stadium. It's like a mine or tunnel. The air in the tunnel is cool as an autumn night. The soft yellow glow of sunlight can be seen at the far end of the passageway. It's as if the light is an approaching freight train.

The sounds of voices drift into the concrete tunnel. The familiar noise of balls striking leather quickens my pace. I can't wait to see where the Barons play.

"Well shut my mouth. I swear half the state of Alabama is here." Mule has nailed it. There must be over a hundred ballplayers spread from one side of the bright green ball field to the other.

Half the players wear over-alls while the others are wearing uniforms bearing the name of their hometown. I count uniforms from Mobile, Tuscaloosa, Rainsville, Montgomery, and just about every town in Walker County.

I turn my attention to surveying the ballpark. A wooden fence, that looks as tall as a schoolyard flagpole, surrounds the field. Signs, some promoting Coke-a-Cola, a drug store, and beer cover every square inch of the fence. One sign with fancy swirling letters is advertising a clothing store. That store promises a free suit to any player who can hit a hole in the fence located at the bottom of the sign.

A large black and white scoreboard is mounted on the fence in left field. I'm amazed at the sight of a large clock mounted on top of the scoreboard. I turn back to examine the stadium. There are enough seats to sit everybody in Walker County.

On the roof of the stadium are lights, each as big as Momma's washtub, and mounted on steel frames. The kettle shaped lights drape over the field along the first and third base lines. What appears to be a church steeple on top of the stadium roof arouses my curiosity. Why is there a steeple on a baseball stadium?

"From the looks of things, you boys must be here for the try-outs?"
The question comes from a fit looking man. He looks like the pictures of Thomas Jefferson. His face is tan as if he's been on a tropical island, and the sun has left his skin looking tight and shiny. He's wearing white baseball trousers with the legs cuffed below the knee. Blue and red socks extend from the bottom of the cuffed pants down to his shoes. He wears a simple, short-sleeved white jersey that's open at the neck. On his head sits a blue hat with a red bill. A large red "C" fills the front of the cap.

"Yes Sir."

He introduces himself. It's Mr. Hank, the coach I spoke to on the telephone.

"You'll need to check in at the table over yonder. That pretty lady will help you get signed up. Just give Miss Fran your name. Once you've finished go play some catch. Limber up your arms. Try-outs will commence in twenty minutes."

I don't know how I missed the large table? It's set next to the ramp where we'd entered the field. A second look leaves me wondering how we missed the young lady standing behind the long table? She is what Mote would call a "dish." Like Katharine Hepburn, she has honey brown hair that bounces and curls around her shoulders. Her painted lips are as red as a ripe melon.

Mule ushers us over to the table. The young woman isn't much older than Sarah Kate or some of the girls at the high school. Her eyes are dark like Hersey's chocolate. Her white dress has a fancy laced collar.

"I'll need to know your name, and where you're from." She is looking at one of the toughest boys I know standing next to the table.

Berl doesn't answer. He is frozen beside the table. He is staring at the young woman as if he expects her to fly or for music to burst from her lips.

"Ya gonna tell her your name, or you act like you never been out of Walker County?"

A crimson shade has burst out on Berl's face. He stutters as he tells the gorgeous brunette his name. "Berrrrrl, Berl, Berl Nelson. Ahhhhhhhhhhhhhhhhhh, Baseball."

Me, and the rest of the Walker boys, are busting a gut. The sparkling smile and long flittering eyelashes has the big bruiser tongue-tied.

"She knows you play baseball. She needs to know where you're from knucklehead."

"Coal Valley. Coal Valley Ma'am."

"Here you are Berl." With long slender fingers she extends a white card to Berl. The card is the size of a man's hand. Painted on the card is 101. "Here, pin it to your shirt so the coaches can identify you during the tryouts."

The girl's hand waits for Berl to accept the pin while he remains frozen at the table. His eyes locked on her deep brown eyes.

"Berl. You gonna stand here all day? We need to sign-up too." With some nudging we finally get Berl to collect the pin and move away from the table.

Once we've shared our names with Miss Fran we move to one of the dugouts that's built under the stadium. As I start to change my shoes I look at my card. Number 95. What's the number suppose to mean? Is the number some form of pecking order? Are there ninety four players better than me here at Rickwood."

"Mule. You think the number means anything?"

"Yep, it means you're an outfielder. Look at Jack's number." I quickly see that Jack card bears the number 39.

"All the first basemen are wearing a card number with thirty something. The numbers tell what position yer playing."

247

"Whew. That's a relief." Charlie lets out a long, deep sigh. He number is 99.

"I got 101. I suppose the one is for pitchers?"

With the mystery of the assigned numbers solved we lace up our baseball spikes. Ready, we head out for some catch. Our spikes make a clacking sound on the hard floor. The noise reminds me of a drummer beating a call to battle.

"You boys gather in the outfield."

I look for the source of the booming voice. I turn my attention to the steeple on top of the grandstands. It's not a steeple, but a booth for announcing the game. I can see a fellow sitting behind what appears to be a desk. The man is wearing a white shirt, tie, and dark trousers. The glare of the late morning sun peaking over the stadium rooftop makes it hard to make out the face.

I join the mob that is trotting into centerfield. We huddle around the slender man who had met us when we came out of the tunnel. Two other men wearing matching Reds uniforms stand beside him. Like Mr. Hank their skin is golden brown and stretched tight across their face.

"Take a knee boys."

There is little conversation as we settle on the outfield. The grass feels soft like one of Momma's quilts. However, unlike some the fields in Walker County there are no rocks. Nor, are there any patches of bare earth. Several of the boys around me are running their hands over the grass as if petting a good dog.

"Welcome to tryouts. The Reds are pleased that you all could make it. We hope that someday you might help the Reds win a pennant. I'm Mr. Hank. I'm a coach for the Reds. No sense in telling you my last name. None of you could spell it. Plus, half of you couldn't say it. Just call me Mr. Hank. Mr. Crossley and Mr. Morrell here, will be evaluating players too." Crossley has thick shoulders. He is about Pap's size. Morrell is a tall lanky fellow with eyes that seem to search our group like a hawk preying on squirrels.

Mr. Hank continues, "Outfielders will work with Mr. Crossley. Mr. Morrell will observe the pitchers. Infielders will report to me."

"Here's the routine for today. Pitchers and catchers will work in the bullpens with Mr. Morrell. For the first half hour infielders will field ground balls while the outfielders chase fly balls. Once the arms are loosening up we'll run through some situations. Last hour this morning will be for batting. Pitchers will be throwing on the sidelines during the batting session. We'll take a lunch break. Finally, we'll have a game. Twenty-four infielders and outfielders will be picked to play in the game. A like number of pitchers will be chosen to throw in the game. After the noon meal we'll post the players who have been selected to play in the game over yonder where Miss Francis signed you in this morning. If there aren't any questions we'll get started."

"Mr. Hank. Looks to be more than twenty-four players here that ain't pitchers. What are the rest of the players doing?" The anxious voice came from somewhere behind me.

"They'll be heading home. Any more questions?"

The massed circle of tryout hopefuls is mum as the meaning of Mr. Hank's word sets in.

"Fine, let play some ball."

The remainder of the morning feels like a fantasy. In the outfield not a single ball escapes my glove as I run them down from every angle. My throws are on target when I fire them back to a waiting infielder. My bat thunders with each pitch that finds the strike zone. Twenty times I send the ball zipping through the infield, or plastering the outfield fence. The morning ends when we're called in for a noon meal.

"What kind of food they serving?"

"It's a hot dog."

A boy from Pumpkin Ridge is looking over the hot dog as if might bite him. Jack's remark seems to put the fellow at ease.

"Heard tell of them. First time I'd ever seen one." I recognize the voice as the one asking Mr. Hank about the other players.

We devour the hot dogs, and sweet tea that has been set out for the ballplayers. I'm amazed at Berl's delight in the mustard. I can hardly see the dog for all the yellow coating. Eventually Berl has as much mustard on his hands and chin as he manages to swallow.

"Look. Mr. Hank is posting the names." There is a stampede as hot dogs are stuffed into mouths, or cast aside. Cups of sweet tea rain over the field as every player makes for the list hanging on a post near the tunnel.

I can't see the list for the bodies that block my path. I squirm forward as the boys in the front take account of the names, and then move away. Some players are prancing back toward the field while others lumber away.

I find three lists. One is labeled Red, another White, and the last Blue. I search for my name. There, I'm on the White team. Jack is also on the White team. I worm my way out of the wall of bodies crushing forward where they hope to see they won't be heading home early. I find my Valley teammates, clustering around Mule, chatting. Charlie is assigned to the Red team. Gus is on the Blue with Berl who's pitching for the Blue squad. All the boys from the Valley will be playing. Mule says he ain't surprised. He'd been watching the morning segment from the grandstands. He had been appraising our performance against the other boys.

"Red team is batting. White team is playing the field. Blue team will rotate to the field once the Red team finishes batting. The White team will bat next." The voice in the steeple finishes the announcement.

"Look sharp. Feel Sharp. Be Sharp." The jingle from a shaving cream company blares over the field. The try-out has taken on a feeling of a big league series.

For the rest of the afternoon I'm in the outfield, batting, or watching the Red and Blue teams square off against one another. While the Red and Blue demonstrate their pitching, fielding, and hitting talents I study the pitchers.

Where is the Bankhead pitcher's release point? The pitcher from Mount Pinson is tipping his in pitch. The heavy bearded pitcher from Tarrant only has one pitch. The boy from Florence is throwing peas.

The game has rotated to where the White team is taking a final turn batting. I hit a line drive to the first baseman on my first turn to bat. My next two turns to bat are hits that pounded against the right field fence. My previous hit barely cleared the fence in center field.

The Florence pitcher with a fire balling arm is pitching. I expect to see a hard straight pitch and nothing else. That pitch is his meal ticket. The rotating seams on the ball prove me right. It's a pea.

The moment the sweet spot of my bat impacts the ball I know it's my best hit of the day. I feel the shock from my fingers all the way to my shoulders. I haven't even reached first base when I see the ball clip the top of a towering tree beyond the fence in right field.

When I cross home plate I take a quick glance at the field. Every member of the Red team is still gazing off where the ball has disappeared. The Florence pitcher wears a slack jawed expression when he turns back toward home plate. My teammates are laughing, and whooping as I trot into the dugout.

Mr. Crossley is shaking his head. His jaw is tilted to one side. His lips are puckered. "Where you learn to hit like that boy?"

"Been hitting corn cobs, and bottle caps since I could walk."

"What? Corn cobs, and bottle caps?" Mr. Crossely never finishes what he's thinking. He merely shakes his head a few more times before turning his attention back to the field.

"What that Mr. Hanks tell ya?"

"We'll get a letter in the mail if we're invited to training in Florida next spring."

"Ya all did real fine." The try-outs are over. We pile back into Mule's Ford for the trip back to The Valley. Mule dissects every at bat, every pitch, and every play we made today. The swaying and rolling motion of the roadster makes keeping my head up a difficult task. I'm tuckered out.

"Hurrah for the Valley." Old Reese's cheer brings me out of my slumber. Like my pals, I fell asleep on the trip home. Old Reese is standing on the Commissary porch. His cigar is between his lips. The brown stogie wobbles from one corner of his mouth to the other. "How we all do Mr. Mule?"

"The boys did real fine Reese. Real fine."

Jack, Berl, and Charlie have been left off at their homes. Mule is motoring up to my home when I see Deacon's Chevrolet parked in front of the house. Why isn't he in Charleston? Then I remember. He's come back for Juanita, and their baby girl Martha.

Mule brakes to a stop next to the Chevrolet. I bound from the Ford, and make for the porch. "Thanks for ride, Mule."

"Today I was sitting in high cotton watching you boys put on a show for the Reds."

I wave as Mule turns the Roadster back down the road toward the Commissary. The door to the house is open. A screen is keeping the skeeters out. I hear my family all-talking at once. "How'd you do?"
"Did you get a big offer?"

"Did you see Mutt Riddle?"

It's five minutes before I can finally get a word out. "Won't know what the Reds thought of me for a few months. They'll be sending a letter if they want me to come to training camp in Florida next spring."

"Well, if the Reds don't need you this season you're going back to Charleston with Juanita and me."

"Why am I going with you and Juanita?"

"The shipyard is hiring. Plenty of jobs to be had."

I know that Pap and Momma will have it easier with one less mouth to feed. The notion of going to Charleston is exciting. It's a chance to make good wages. What about school? No, I got enough credit to graduate early.

"Go fetch your things."

"Other than a pair of over-alls, he's wearing his things." Momma didn't even look up from her sewing with that statement.

It's a fact. Everything I owned I put in a paper sack for the trip to Charleston. Five minutes later, having hugged Momma, shook Pap's hand, and threw wisecracks at Tut and Jesse, I'm on my way to Charleston. We leave the Valley under a black sky and distant stars. The silver glow of the moon is popping up over the hilltops as the lights of the Valley disappear.

Deacon is driving while Juanita is cradling their baby girl in her arms. I'm curled up in the backseat thinking about today, and Rickwood Field. Whether the Reds want me, or not, it was the best day ever. I fall asleep in the Chevrolet before we reach the Warrior River.

Chapter 28
"Farewell to the Valley"

"WAR."

That was the newspapers headlines in Charleston ten months ago. I'd been working with a grinder that Sunday when word spread around the shipyard that our Pacific fleet had been attacked. My foreman, Sam, declared, "Cuz, them boys just kicked a sleeping bear. Gonna come the day when they'll wish they never heard of the good old USA."

Sam is an old country boy from Macon, Georgia. He is thick as a rain barrel. His hairline has receded to the point where it was invisible. I swear he's over seventy. He walks with a shuffle, and his body sags as he moves around the ship. He'd plowed with mules, cut pine trees for sawmills, and worked in shipyards. Despite a body that had been worn down from years of demanding work Sam can outwork most of the men in our section. I don't recall ever seeing Sam without his corncob pipe. Even when he wasn't smoking, the pipe was anchored between his teeth.

Once Mr. Roosevelt got a declaration of war, every soul in the country seemed to be joining the military, or the Civil Defense program. Sam prompted me to consider staying on at the shipyard, "Cuz, this shipbuilding is gonna get hotter than a goats bottom in a pepper patch."

As soon as I turned eighteen, I gave notice at the shipyard. I intended on enlisting despite Sam's pledging that "your duties in the shipyard would be classified as essential to the war effort." I can't let my brothers and pals go off to war while I stay behind. I don't want to shirk my duty to serve Uncle Sam. The idea of being labeled a "draft dodger" just doesn't sit well with me.

In what has become a family tradition, I enlisted in the Navy in Charleston. Five days later me and hundred other boys were on a train bound for Memphis. The train arrived that afternoon in Tennessee where the Memphis recruit depot was overflowing with more boys like me. Like my first hunt with Pap's rifle, my day at the depot was like an illusion. I'm filled with apprehension and bewilderment. I was herded along with the army of fellow recruits through the installation. The Navy depot was built like a warehouse. Inside the atmosphere resembled a nosey carnival midway packed with anxious and dazed people.

I'll bet there were more doctors in the depot than in the state of Alabama. Me, and all the other fellows, spent a good spell naked from the waist up. The doctors took our pulse, examined our eyes, checked our ears, and thumped our chest. Next thing you know, they're told us to drop our drawers. I swear some of them boys looked and smelled as if they'd never hear of soap and water.

When the doctors weren't peeking, and probing, we sat with typists. These clerks wore uniforms of every branch of the military. The questions came rapid fire. The typewriters clack, ding, and whump as we revealed our personal history. Like men on trial we're bombarded with questions about parents, family, jobs, schooling, whether we had knowledge of firearms, did we know any individual living in a country hostile to the United States, use alcohol to excess, and if we attended church?

The last two hours we squeezed into a big auditorium. Once we were seated we took every reading, writing, and math test devised by high school teachers. I felt bad for some boys that couldn't read nor write. The officer in charge told those fellows to mark an X on each form. Once the X was made another man would fill in the name next to the X.

When the Navy was finished I hopped the train bound for home. I'm to report back to the Memphis depot for a swearing in ceremony in ten days.

With what's left of my last, shipyard wages, rolled and stuffed in my pocket, I arrived home packing "Half and Half" pipe tobacco and "Red Man" for Pap.

For Momma I carry a new, straw hat that's flush with pink and white bows. I found a hatpin in the "Five and Dime" store to go with the hat. A large white bead, shaped like a flower, is mounted on top of the pinhead. It's good to see Momma smile even if just for a moment.
Tut and Jesse devour the box of "Cracker Jacks" they discovered in the extravagant booty I picked up in Oakman.

Her chair squeaks and moans as Momma rocks and forth on the porch this morning. Daylight had revealed the first frost of autumn. Now, the sunshine is pushing the cool morning air aside. Momma has thrown a shawl over shoulders. The needle in her hands darts through the fabric as she sews. Maybe it's a shirt for Pap, or nightshirt for little Joy. Her eyes shift after each stitch monitoring the activities of my little sister Joy, corralled on the porch. Joy plays with a doll that Momma made. The doll is made from an old sock with black buttons for the eyes and nose. Heavy red cord forms the lips and hair. The doll is never far from my little sister.

When she's not glancing at Joy, Momma searches the road for Mr. Hanby making his rounds with the daily mail. Tut revealed that every morning for the pass five months Momma settles into that rocking chair. With Joy playing at her feet she waits for the postmaster to arrive. For Momma, every letter received from Chip and Mote offers one more day of hope that her prayers are being answered. Each letter prompts a smile that disappears as quickly as a drop of water on a hot skillet.

The days have vanished like a sunset. Today, as Jesse and I play catch in front of the house I steal peeks at Momma. For the first time I notice streaks of grey spouting in her coal black hair. The wrinkles on her face, once small and subdued like those on a baby's hand, now resemble small furrows. The lines speak volumes for the hard times in the Valley. Creases on her forehead betray the valiant façade she has thrown up to shield her from the hostile images of war that threatens our family and the nation.

The radio and newspapers offer little encouragement. In the Pacific our boys are fighting with their backs to the wall. In the last year, Wake Island and the Philippines have fallen to the onslaught of Japanese forces. Like fire in dry tinder, word had quickly spreads that Berl's brother has been taken captive in the Philippines.

Nazi U-boats roam the Atlantic marauding through the shipping lanes seeking to isolate the nation from our allies. Nightfall leaves the nation dark as blackouts are ordered due to the fear of bombing raids such as the English are enduring. Chip is somewhere in the Atlantic. Mote is on the West coast where he is soon to ship out for places unknown.

Many of my classmates have departed for military service. The Oakman school board established an early graduation for boys eligible for military service so as they could graduate and enlist in the service. Berl enlisted in the Marine Corp as soon as he turned eighteen. My pal, who throws a baseball with such velocity it appeared like a comet speeding across the sky and drew scrutiny from a trainload of professional scouts, has enlisted. He is determined that his brother wouldn't be the only Nelson to join the fight.

Conky and Runt, like Mote, have left for duty with the Navy. Margaret, Jack's sister, brought news of Jack's enlistment in the Army. I was still seventeen when our class graduated. I had to wait until I reached the qualifying age for enlistment.

War has changed Coal Valley. Daily activities no longer yield to darkness. The mines run night and day. Trainloads of Valley coal highball to the Birmingham mills two or three times a day.

I grew up in the Valley. Yet, I encounter so many new faces as I walk the road I feel like a stranger. Poking my head into the Commissary, or passing by the schoolhouse, I feel lost. I'm like a stick in the water being carried off by the current. A good many of my classmates are gone. Most of the boys have left for the military. Some of the fellas have been classified 4F. They are working in the mines. There's rumor of a couple of boys lying low so as not to have to explain why they haven't joined up. The girls are gone too. They're working in factories or off to prepare, sort, and organize the bloated piles of paperwork exploding in the nation's capital and military bases that have mushroomed around the country.

Just as stars can be seen hanging in the windows of French Camp, the Flats, and Silk Stocking Hill, they also appear in windows of Black Camp. The Valley's Black Team's first baseman, Dan Gardner, who could field errant throws with the swiftness of a hawk, has joined up with the Army.

Searching for news of my pals, I sought out Jack's sister Margret, Berl's folks, and Conky's father. Margret fidgets as she describes the latest letters from Jack as he described his training in Georgia. He's jumping out of airplanes. Some thing's never change. Jack was fearless on the base paths. He never shied away from sliding headfirst. Now jumping out of airplanes doesn't seem like a stretch for Jack.

Berl's folks share the latest news from their Marine. Berl's letters are full of rumors, or scuttlebutt as he calls it. The letters include speculation that the Marines are bound for Wake Island where they intend on retaking the island. Others rumors include an invasion of Japan itself, or shipping off to the European front. Berl mentions that the scuttlebutt changes every time the Gunny orders a smoke break.

Conky's phone calls and letters home aren't much different than those from Mote. Seems like the sailors spend a good deal of time learning that the Navy has it's own language. A door is a hatch, a kitchen is a galley, and cup of coffee is a cup of Joe. Like Mote, Conky can't believe the Navy has so many ways to tie a knot.

I ventured over to Oakman, and the high school. Coach Gibson has been called to duty. He has been given a Navy commission and is serving as a fitness instructor. I recall the football practices that Coach conducted. Sure as shooting there'd be some miserable sailors when Coach Gibson gets hold of their sorry bodies. I wonder if I'll cross paths with him somewhere down the line?

When I'm not playing catch with Jesse I spend time with Pap and Tut. We walk the steep hills. We wander up the creek branches squirrel hunting. Pap and I carry rifles. Tut totes his weapon of choice, a trusty slingshot.

It's my last Saturday in the Valley before I board the train back to Memphis. Pap is working in one of the mines. Tut and I are alone in the hills where we hope to find a squirrel or two with the intent of filling a pot for Momma. Tut waste no time in putting me to shame as he bags a squirrel before I can shoulder my rifle. Tut is grinning and taunting.

"How ya all gonna help win the war if ya can be outgunned by a slingshot?" I quickly dismiss Tut's jabs and sarcastic humor. I begin to anticipate supper, relishing the idea of Momma fixing a stew simmering with squirrel and dumplings.

"All the same to me. Long as there's a squirrel in the stew it don't matter how he came to be there."

Tut begins to run down the hill with his slingshot bouncing in one hand. The squirrel's fuzzy body is flopping in the other. "Well maybe I'll tell Momma to put off fixing any squirrel stew until you get on that train back to Memphis."

With his spirited head start, and me carrying Pap's rifle, I have as much of chance of catching Tut as I do of catching a hummingbird. After a short spell I give up the chase, shoulder the rifle and drift down the hillside.

The foliage is thick. Sunbeams trickle down between the leaves. Pine trees sag, as each limb is burden with cones. The ash, birch, and oak trees cast a canopy of bright colors overhead. The hills of Walker County appear to be on fire as autumn nudges summer aside.

I no longer hear Tut's laughter as he disappears further into the creek bottom. The air is silent. Working in the shipyard I've been exposed to endless noise. For the past months my world has been filled with pounding hammers, the clamor of powerful drills, and hearty voices.

Here in the hills around the Valley I find solitude in the tranquil sounds of the hills, woods, and creeks. I listen to the sounds of an old gray pine; its bark no longer protects it's soft core. The proud old tree creaks in the wind. It waits for the storm that will rip it from free from an eternity spent on the hillside

The wind whispers through the leaves and boughs of the trees. Across the creek another squirrel chatters like a frantic mother. The creek bed gurgles as water flows from pool, to rock, and down into the next pool.

I resume following the creek as it meanders through the steep ravine. My pace is slow and deliberate. For the first time I think about war. I wonder about life aboard a warship. I try to imagine the chaos, the noise, and the unknown. Will I ever walk the hills again? Will I ever again see Pap, Momma, and my brothers?

A shadow in the trees catches my attention. A squirrel is darting from tree to tree. Its leaps are effortless and graceful. I watch the squirrel bound from one tree to another. I forget the rifle cradled in my arms as the squirrel romps through the treetops.

"What ya doing?" Tut has retraced his path. He is apparently puzzled by my lack of pursuit.

"Listening."

"Listening to what?"
"The silence."
"Silence doesn't make a sound."

"It does if you stop and think about it"

"Them Navy folks up in Memphis, they know about your hearing problems?"

Again, Tut is running with me on his heels. The thought of squirrel stew urges me to pick up the pace. By the time the house comes into view the run through the hills has me feeling invigorated and peaceful.

That evening when Momma calls us to supper the table feels deserted. Spots along the bench that were once filled by my brothers are vacant. Memories of their voices and laughter taunt me during supper. Despite being surrounded by two younger brothers, my sister, Pap, and Momma, I am overcome with loneliness.

"Momma tells me that we're eating stew courtesy of Tut?" Pap is looking at me.

"Yep, we best let FDR know that a slingshot in Tut's hand could be a secret weapon that will put the fear of God in old Adolph."

Later there is no brother hogging the bed. Like me, Jesse and Tut sleep alone. There is no brother to pull the covers off. No brother taking his half of the bed out of the middle. The room is as black as the coalmines in which Pap works. A cricket's creaking breaks the silence.

I feel for the letter folded up beneath my pillow. I've been invited to spring training with the Reds. This war has sure interrupted my plans. No spring training. The lifetime dream of wearing a professional baseball uniform seems so far away. So many of my pals, cousins, and brothers have seen dreams interrupted by the needs of our nation.

The cricket creaks again. I wonder if the cricket is as naïve about the coming winter as I'm of going to war?

I toss around in the bed. I slug the heavy down filled pillow with the violence of a Jack Dempsey punch. I fall asleep imagining the thumping sound of my foot slapping second base. My cap is soaring off in my wake. My arms are pumping vigorously as they brush my ribs. My chin is down, and my eyes monitor the actions of the Brooklyn infielder.

I catch the gestures of coach Hank as I stretch a double into a triple.

The remaining time passes quickly. Today Pap and I walked up, down, and across the hills of the Valley. When we finally arrive at our destination Pap points out the gnarly oak tree. It's his bee tree. One afternoon Pap spotted a bee squatting in the cool mud of a fishing hole in Black Creek. Pap gathered up his homemade pole and followed the bee into the hills and to the oak tree's cavity. A winter wind had pulled a limb free creating a gigantic hole. The massive hole was now the site of a humming and swarming beehive. Pap will smoke the hive and retrieve the honey in the coming days.

We settle down on a smooth, barren log and watch the activity around the hive, quietly observing the industrial ways of the bees. Then Pap says,

"You and your brothers have had a tough go of it here in Coal Valley. There was never enough to eat. You never had enough warm clothes come winter. You survived tough times. You and your brothers will survive this war. God willing."

This evening I counted seventeen dollars left from my shipyard wages. I set two dollars aside for my trip. The house is quiet and dark as I ease into the kitchen being careful not to bang any pots, or pans, nor bump any chairs. With the caution of a fox raiding a hen house I grope amongst the kitchen shelves until I find Momma's money jar. Easing the lid off I take the remaining fifteen dollars and fold it into the jar.

My time at home is over. Mule, in his black Ford, is parked in front of the house. The Valley's baseball manager waits to take me to the train depot in Oakman. Pap is back in the mine. Tut has caught the bus to Oakman and the high school. Jesse is wearing my old Barons ball cap when Mr. Dutton began his bell ringing, then Jesse hurries off for school. We did squeeze in one final game of catch before he answered the summons.

Momma's hug almost takes the breath out of me as we say good-bye. Her eyes glisten. I swallow hard fighting back a tear. I pick up the brown paper sack that holds a change of underwear and a toothbrush. I solemnly make my way down the porch steps, and crawl into the coupe. Mule nods as the engine roars to life. The Ford lunges forward. I wave good-bye to Momma. We head to the Oakman train depot and the war.

The coupe bumps down the road. Passing the ball field I think of Mr. Ozzie. As we approach the Commissary the image of my pals hiding under the porch, racing down the road on horseback, or listening to Uncle Cullie's radio materializes before my eyes.

I recognize the rickety old wagon and frail horse standing near the road. The Valley's number one baseball fan is perched on the long porch. The skinny black man leans against one of the large wooden post. The signature cigar juts from a corner of his mouth. As the Ford draws even with the Commissary he straightens up, and frees the cigar from its clinches. His eyes search and find mine. He waves and cheers.

"Hurrah for the Valley. Hurrah for the Valley Mr. Spike."

I return the wave as I recall Pap's words, "You and your brothers are survivors." Someday I will return to the Valley.

Epilogue

Many of the proofreaders for "Hurrah for The Valley" books recommended that an epilogue be included to bring closure to the story. As my father's story concluded in early 1942, the idea of a complete epilogue has proven almost impossible. Many of the book's characters had left Walker County during WWII and never returned. Unfortunately, many of the characters have passed away, leaving no information as to their personal history after 1942. The absence of information on many of The Valley's grand personalities such as Big John Shelton, Old Reese Edinburg, Lewis and Hazel Ary, Bud Millwood, and many more is regretted.

Clyde (Spike) Powell participated in five island invasions during WWII. He moved to Oregon after the war. He played semi-professional baseball until 1954, and never lost his eye for hitting as he had a .302 batting average and didn't strike out once in his final three seasons. He worked for the Spokane, Portland, & Seattle railroad until it merged with Burlington Northern. He served as an advisor to the regional vice president. He and his wife Mary had three children, and four grandchildren, and five great grandchildren. He died in 2013 and was carried back to Alabama to be buried in the family plot in Walker County.

Conley (Chip) Powell was a WWII and veteran of the war in the Pacific. Following WWII Chip became a compulsion engineer. Chip and Margie had two daughters, five grandchildren, and 13 great grandchildren. Chip died in 2007 and is buried in Winfield, Kansas.

Charles (Deacon) Powell moved to California after WWII. where he was a foreman in the transportation industry.

Deacon and Juanita had three children and five grandchildren. Following his retirement Deacon returned to Alabama, built a home on lake front property where he could fish everyday. He passed away in 2006

Cullman (Mote) Powell chose to remain in the US Navy after WWII. He retired a after twenty years of service to his country. His Navy tour took him from the invasion of Normandy in 1944 to peacetime duty in Japan. Following his career in the Navy Mote went on to a career as a industrial contractor. He retired to Walker County where he could fish, hunt, and share his woodworking talents with neighbors and family. Mote passed away in 2009. He is buried in the National Cemetery in Birmingham.

Clay (Tut) Powell lives in Goldendale, Alabama. He celebrated his 91 birthday on Memorial Day, 2017. During WWII Tut served in the US Navy in the Atlantic Theater. He was a veteran of the North Africa invasion. After his discharge, Tut returned to Oakman High School and completed his high school education. Tut is married to Carolyn (Davison) and has two boys. Tut served as an agent for the Pure Oil Company until his retirement. He remains a true Crimson Tide fan. Without his support and contributions this book would have never be completed.

Clarence (Jesse) Powell - like his brothers, also served in the US Navy. A veteran of the Korean War, he joined Spike in Oregon and worked for the railroad. Jesse continued to play baseball and fast pitch softball well into his 30's. He eventually returned to Alabama where he worked for the US Postal Service. He and his wife Joan have three children, and one grandchild. Jesse passed away in November of 2016. Jesse was a key resource in the writing of "Hurrah for The Valley." He is buried in Walker County.

Joy (Powell) Taylor - She and her husband Roy eventually settled in Walker County when Roy retired from the US Air Force. They have two surviving children, and four grandchildren. Joy is active with her church and the Senior Center. Like her mother, Joy's quilts are the source of family pride and envy. Much of the last chapters from Book 2 are based upon her memories. Ironically, it was not until she was in her twenty's that she finally sat at supper with all her siblings surrounding her.

Jack Houk (aka Hauck) - The dare devil ball player that joined Spike and The Valley ball team every summer, served in the 82nd Airborne during WWII. Jack participated in combat jumps in North Africa, Anzio, and Normandy. Jack was killed in action on June 6th, 1944 while serving as a pathfinder for his Battalion.

Col. George Earnest (Runt) - After serving in the Navy during WWII, he enlisted in the U.S. Army. During his distinguished career, he served in Korea and Vietnam and ended his career at the Pentagon; He died in 2009 and is interred at Arlington. For 59 years, he was married to Valley girl Marionette Lockhart.

Burl Nelson returned to Alabama after serving in the US Marine Corp during WWII. Burl survived some of the most vicious combat in the Pacific. He continued to play semi professional baseball long after the war.

John Julian – the tremendous ball player from Sipsey enlisted in the Army and served with the 101st Airborne. Julian was attached to Easy Company of the 506, which became known as the "Band of Brothers." Julian was killed in action at the Battle of the Bulge (1945).

Conky Jones: Like most of his generation that lived in Walker County during the Great Depression, Conky also served in the military during WWII. He eventually moved to Phoenix, Arizona. He and Spike remained friends throughout their life time. Phone calls were common, and occasionally they found time to meet during reunions and vacations that were filled with laughter and story telling. Conky's younger brother Pud was killed in an accident while attempting to rescue two small boys. The Jones brothers were named Cornell and Auburn, but their friends referred to them by their nicknames.

Johnnie Cicero-In 1942, he took a job at Praco Mine in Jefferson County. He played there in '42 and was killed there in a mining accident the same year.

Gus Cicero-After WWII, he briefly played at North Alabama University. He played baseball at Corona and Gorgas Mine for a couple of years. He retired after a distinguished career with the Alabama Department of Transportation and died soon after retirement.

Brother Turner (Rex) - A few years after Coal Valley, he helped found, what is now, Faulkner University in Montgomery. He was a renowned theologian, educator and civic leader. He died in 2001.

Drew Gibson (Coach) - began his head-coaching career at Curry in 1932-33. He was at Walker in 1934 and Carbon Hill in '35. He came to Oakman in 1936 and remained through 1944. After a stint in the Navy, he returned to Oakman as principal and remained there until he retired.

Coach Gibson had undefeated seasons at Carbon Hill and at Oakman in 1940.

Sara Kate Bagwell - married Paul Gwinn and lived a long and rewarding life in Walker County. To her family and friends she was one of county's most elegant ladies.

Frank Corry - he served in the US Navy during WWII as a Navy medic, Frank was attached to the USMC during some of the most horrific battles in the Pacific Theater. Upon his return to Oakman, Frank was introduced to, and eventually married one of his mother's students, Nell Schultz. Nell's brothers were key characters in much of the book. Frank and Nell settled in Georgia. They have two children, two grandchildren, and five great grandchildren.

Virgil Ledbetter-the Dora pitcher was the longtime baseball and basketball coach at Samford University and assistant football coach to Bobby Bowden. He was a Dodger scout. He died in 1967.

Loel Passe - attended Parrish High School and probably graduated in 1935. The voice for the local theater houses went on to become an announcer for the Birmingham Barons baseball club where the owner of the Houston Astros discovered him. In 1960 Passe became a member of the Houston broadcast team. Loel died in 1997 and is buried in Walker County near his parents and siblings.

Johnny Dove-He was too old for WWII service so he went north to work in a defense plant. He never returned to the south.

Carbon Hill running back Lloyd Cheatham was an All-SEC back at Auburn who played minor league baseball. He played in the NFL before and after WWII. He passed away in 1987.

Junior Dunn - The Empire player signed with the Birmingham Barons in 1941 and played minor league ball before and after WWII service. He presently lives in Sheffield, AL.

Buck and Bobby Julian-They played three years of minor league ball together after WWII. Buck was a business owner and served as Mayor of Sipsey. He passed away in 1999. Bobby retired from the Alabama Power Company and resides in Jasper.

Proof

Made in the USA
Columbia, SC
04 July 2017